PRESENTED TO:

Hope Leroy

FROM:

Sheed Conner

DATE:

Dec 3, 2023

This was written by my
Niece I hope you Enjoy

Endorsements

"Every day, life leads us down different roads, and yet it's the sufficiency of God's amazing grace that accompanies us. In *Grace for the Day*, Pam Workman has prepared an incredible master road map for the journey."

Jamie Tuttle
Lead Pastor
Dwelling Place Church

"Everyone needs this book as a go-to book just to stay encouraged. *Grace for the Day* is life changing and healing! It is for you on those days when you need a reminder or pick me up! Great Encouragement!"

"Real Talk" Kim Jones
Senior Pastor, Limitless Church

Grace for the Day is a delightful gift of inspiration! Each day's reading provides a glimpse of grace through personal examples, encouraging scriptures, and thought-provoking questions for reflection. A beautiful reminder of God's lovingkindness, *Grace for the Day*, is the ideal gift for someone you love or as a daily encouragement for your soul.

Dr. Shelia Cornea
Leadership Coach

Xulon Press Elite
555 Winderley Pl, Suite 225
Maitland, FL 32751
407.339.4217
www.xulonpress.com

Paperback ISBN-13: 978-1-66286-909-9
Ebook ISBN-13: 978-1-66286-910-5

FOREWORD BY JUDY JACOBS

GRACE

for the Day

An Uncommon Grace for an Uncommon Life

31 Days of Grace

·Pamela Conner Workman, Ed.S·

XULON ELITE

Dedication

I DEDICATE THIS BOOK to those who have gone before us and those living among us who have given their lives for the cause of Jesus Christ. Many people have been martyred giving their last breaths to spread the Gospel of Jesus Christ. May our lives reflect their sacrifices, intense perseverance, passion, and hearts to carry the gospel of truth throughout the world. These people radically trusted God and in His power to provide unlikely, supernatural results. We saw Peter and John pray until the building where they were gathered began to shake. And they were all filled with the Holy Spirit and spoke the Word of God boldly (see Acts 4:31, NIV). "When they saw the courage of Peter and John and realized that they were unschooled, ordinary (common) men, they were astonished, and they took note that these men had been with Jesus" (Acts 4:13, NIV). These were common, ordinary men, living uncommon, extraordinary lives because of the gospel of Jesus Christ.

It is the lives of missionaries, ordinary men, and women, doing exploits, going to the furthest corners of the earth, carrying the saving knowledge of Jesus Christ as Savior; common men and women, living extraordinary lives, for the sake of bringing the Good News of Jesus Christ to those who otherwise would not know Jesus Christ as their Savior. By the grace of God, they are world changers and influencers of nations. It is the pastors, ordinary men, and women, leading and discipling their churches to follow Jesus, bringing change in their lives, their marriages, their families, and the community; they are ordinary men and women living extraordinary lives. It is the mother, father, teacher, businessperson, friend, ordinary men, and women, who have given their hearts and lives to live a life that reflects Jesus

Christ and through their ordinary circumstances bring the gospel to their world. It is through God's grace these ordinary people living extraordinary lives in the harvest fields where God has placed them, bring life and hope to those desperate for a Savior.

Grace is the free and unmerited favor of God, as manifested in the salvation of sinners and the bestowal of blessings. Mercy is compassion or forgiveness given from someone who has the power to punish or forgive. Grace is responsible for the empty grave. May our lives reflect the mercy and grace God has given us through the life of Jesus Christ and through His death and resurrection, taking our sins and extending forgiveness to us.

May we show mercy in all circumstances, forgiving others as Jesus has forgiven us. May we as ordinary (common) people live extraordinary (uncommon) lives through the grace we find in our relationship with Jesus Christ. "Let us then with confidence draw near to the throne of grace, that we may receive mercy and find grace to help in time of need" (Heb. 4:16, ESV).

"For from His fullness we have all received, grace upon grace" (John 1:16, ESV).

Acknowledgments

A T THE END of the Conference for the International Institute of Mentoring, there was a time of impartation. Pastor Jamie Tuttle spoke prophetically to me that I would write a book. This devotional is the beginning of the fulfillment of that prophecy. Thank you, Pastor Jamie, for letting God use you to catapult me to this new season, for hearing the voice of God and helping to guide me in this process. Your knowledge and expertise have been a blessing. Your love and kindness to us has been overwhelming! I will be forever thankful to God for placing you and your family in our lives.

I would like to extend a heartfelt thanks and with much gratitude for the late hours my precious mentor and pastor, Judy Jacobs Tuttle, spent reading over these pages and giving me first words of encouragement and then words of expertise and experience. I have been a student in this process, and I have learned much! I am thankful for the kind and gentle push from her to make the words on each page resound with a message that would touch your heart. I thank her with all my heart for the kindness she has bestowed on me. I am overwhelmed by the goodness of God to allow me to go on this journey and to have such a wonderful mentor and pastor to go along with me. Once again, she has humbled me, and I have been overtaken by the goodness of God by the foreword she wrote for this devotional. If you read only that portion of this book, you would understand the grace of God from the words of a truly extraordinary woman.

Kathy Kennemer, thank you for reviewing portions of this book and giving me helpful suggestions and gentle encouragement. Your life is a true reflection of God's grace and compassion. You amaze me with your willingness to give and pour into so many. Thank you for being an uncommon woman living an uncommon life that reflects the Gospel and grace of Jesus Christ.

Dr. Shelia Cornea, you have been a mentor and friend, who I greatly respect. Thank you for reviewing portions of this book and sharing your expertise, time, words of advice, and encouragement. You are a woman with "gutsy grace," who mentors and lives an intentional life that brings glory to God.

My deepest appreciation to Xulon Publishers for your expertise and encouragement throughout each step of the publishing process. From the cover to the bibliography and all steps in between, I was encouraged, and I am confident that God was leading us in the process.

Finally, I would like to thank my husband, Joe, for his patience during the writing process. Thank you, Joe, for walking along by my side in this journey of life, for loving me, and always being there for me. I would like to thank my sons and their wives and grandchildren for allowing me to share their stories in this devotional.

Foreword

THERE ARE MANY ways to describe something so beautiful as the grace of God. The definition that always stands out to a lot of us is, "the unmerited, unearned love and favor of Almighty God, our Father." I guess there have been many who have written and probably succeeded, but the author of this beautiful devotional, *Grace for the Day*, knows a lot about this particular word as a means of experiencing it on a very personal level. The stories and the testimonies that Pam shares will melt your heart with faith, courage, and assurance that you can trust your Father God to be exactly who He says He will be.

There will be times as you read this book this year that you will be faced with decisions of believing for "Sustaining Grace, Radical Grace, Forgiving Grace," or how about this one, "Grace under Fire." But I also know that when those times come, there will be a "Gift of Grace, A Touch of Grace, A Glorious Grace," and, an "Anointed Grace" to just highlight some of this incredible revelation coming straight from the throne of God and from "the pen of a ready writer" (Ps. 45:1).

As you read this beautiful devotional, *Grace for the Day*, my prayer is that the words on these pages will penetrate you so deeply in the grace and the love of Christ that you will be unshakeable in your faith. Always remember, "For it is by grace you have been saved, through faith—and this is not from yourselves, it is the gift of God—not by works, so that no one can boast" (Eph. 2:8–9).

Paul describes this grace as, "God is able to make all grace (emphasis mine) abound to you so that in all things at all times, having all that you need, you will abound in every good work" (2 Cor. 9:8). I know that as you read these words you will be encouraged, as I have been, to trust Him in the good times and the bad times. You will hear a voice behind you saying, "This is the way walk ye in it" (Isa. 30:21). You can trust your good shepherd that He will not fail you or leave, but His grace will be there to carry you.

As you partake in this spiritual journey of relying on His grace, there are many waters that you can partake in over these next days and weeks, and I pray that by the end of these words of prophetic utterance, that you will be swimming in the grace of Almighty God that Ezekiel the prophet found himself in (Ezek. 47).

Be transformed as you drink deeply in the revelations of the many graces of God that is at your disposal as His child.

Judy Jacobs
Psalmist, Author, Pastor, and Mentor

Introduction

GRACE FOR THE DAY is a thirty-one-day daily devotional. It is a devotional book designed to enhance your daily walk with God. The intent of this devotional is that you will grow in grace and understanding of truth that will empower you to live victoriously and that you will be encouraged and provoked to daily walk out the truth revealed in the Bible. This revelation will provide insight to your understanding of God's ways and nature. God's very character is revealed through the scriptures. As you walk out your personal journey with God, may His Word, as revealed through this devotional, provide guidance to help you navigate through life. As He reveals Himself to you; it will become even more evident that grace can only come from an omnipotent, all-knowing God. He is a sovereign God with sovereign grace. We are justified through faith; this is the miracle of His grace.

Whether working in the marketplace, pursuing a career or ministry, volunteering, or taking care of your family, we all need God's uncommon grace working in our lives. We must have a first-hand, personal, saving knowledge of our Savior and have His uncommon, divine, saving grace changing our lives. My desire is that you will grow in grace and understanding of God as He is revealed through His Word to you and that God's uncommon grace will infiltrate every aspect of your life. Throughout this journey you will see the life stories of common men and women of the Bible whose lives were transformed through an uncommon grace that impacted the course of history. You will also read personal accounts of God's uncommon grace infiltrating lives and miraculously changing circumstances.

We have been called to be change agents to humanity and influencers of nations. We are to fulfill His calling to go forth into the harvest fields and tell others of the saving grace of Jesus Christ. Everybody wants the power and anointing, but all are not willing to pay the price. We are called to live with intentionality and purpose to fulfill the God assignment on our lives. Intentionality and purpose activate us to reach out to others. It propels us to action. It is my hope this devotional will guide you in an uncommon walk with our Savior that leads to an uncommon life and that you will be transformed from the ordinary to the extraordinary.

> "From the fulness of His grace we have all received one blessing after another. For the law was given through Moses, grace and truth came through Jesus Christ" (John 1:16–17, NIV).

Pamela Conner Workman, Ed. S

Table of Contents

"For from his fullness we have all received, grace upon grace" (John 1:16, ESV).

"And He said unto me, 'My grace is sufficient for thee: for my strength is made perfect in weakness.' Most gladly therefore will I rather glory in my infirmities, that the power of Christ may rest upon me" (2 Cor. 12:9, KJV).

DAY 1

Resolute Grace

I LIVED MOST OF my life along the Gulf Coast. I have many wonderful memories of time spent at the beach, sitting along the edge of the water. I would take a piece of driftwood and write in the wet sand. Then the tide would come in and wash away what I had written. This is how it is with Jesus; we all have sin in our hearts until we repent and release it to Him. Then He washes it away and covers it with His resolute grace.

During my second year of college, living in the dorms, I often woke up about two or three o'clock in the morning. I sat on the stairs next to my dorm room, reading my Bible and praying. Early one morning, a young lady and her boyfriend came down the stairs above me. I saw her and could see she was embarrassed for me to see her in this circumstance. I quickly looked away and went into my room, so she would not have to walk past me. We never spoke of that night. When I would see her on campus, I would greet her with a smile and a prayer in my heart.

She left school and went home at the end of the semester. Two and half years later, on my graduation day, this young lady came to me. She said, "I have been looking for you. I came to tell you how grateful I am for you. I know you saw me that night coming downstairs late with my boyfriend, and you knew of my lifestyle. But you never judged me, and you were always kind to me. I want you to know, I saw the love of Jesus in you. I went home at the end of that semester and gave my life back to the Lord. I changed the way I was living. I saw in you what I wanted in my own life. Thank you for showing me the way back to the Lord."

It is never too late to begin this journey or to get back on the right path. The Word of God and your testimony is the solution. How you live should draw others to Jesus. Declare the solutions as the scripture says: "And they overcame him by the blood of the Lamb, and by the word of their testimony; and they loved not their lives unto the death" (Rev. 12:11, KJV). We must live our lives with resolute clarity and resolute grace so that our lives will reveal the love of God and draw others to Him.

We must have the tenacity, resolute grace, to pursue the call of God on our lives. May our passion overcome our fears that we might fully pursue God. As David said, "O Lord, you have searched me, and you know me." God knows everything about us, even our best-kept secrets. As David said: "You know when I sit and when I rise; you perceive my thoughts from afar. You discern my going out and my lying down; you are familiar with all my ways. Before a word is on my tongue you know it completely, O Lord. You hem me in behind and before; and you lay your hand upon me. Such knowledge is too wonderful for me, too lofty for me to attain" (Ps. 139:1–6, NIV).

The scripture from Psalm 139 assures us that God is with us, covers us, and protects us. The Psalmist reveals how God knows us, searches our hearts, and discerns our ways. May our ways lead others to know our Savior. We declare dangerous declarations that bring resolute clarity and grace in our lives and the lives of others.

I have two sons. When they were young and throughout their teen years, many times God would awaken me during the early morning hours. I would go to my boys' rooms and lay on the floor outside their rooms and pray for them. When they were not at home, I would pray over every part of their rooms and even anoint their beds with oil. They never knew I was praying for them during these times; but many times, I saw God's grace extended to them, saving them from car accidents, keeping them from bad influences, and God bringing godly people into their lives. God was working in them during those early years, putting dreams and hope into their hearts.

How wonderful it is that God positions His holy presence to watch over us and cover us even when the darkness surrounds us. I have heard it said, the strongest people are not those who show strength in front of us, but those who win the battles we know nothing about. We are to spend time on our knees to be influencers and to leave a legacy of prayer. It is our time spent in prayer that brings change and victory.

I could see God putting His hand on the shoulders of my boys just as God laid His hand on David. The Psalmist says, "He has laid His hand upon me" (Ps. 139:5, ESV). This speaks of favor and a position of honor. It was a reminder to King David that he had not been forgotten. It is in these times we must lean in to hear God, and our relationship becomes more intimate with Him. God honored, loved, and showed favor to David.

David had a heart after God. In the beginning of this scripture, David states that God has already searched our hearts. He has seen us through His piercing eyes and has investigated our souls. He knows everything about us. God knows the motives, intentions, and the attitudes of our hearts (see Ps. 139, NIV). What I love about God is that He knows if the intentions of our hearts are pure and draws us to His ways. There is nowhere we can run from His presence. He knows what motivates us and how we act and react to situations. God knows every word we are going to speak before we speak it because He knows our hearts just like He knew David's heart.

My boys faced battles of heartaches and loss along the way, and they were challenged to walk in God's resolute grace, with clarity and tenacity, making choices that would bend them toward their destiny. They found resolute clarity and grace for each situation. You may find yourself going through a difficult time. It is God's presence in our lives that enables us to make the right decisions while we hold fast to Him with resolute grace. As we begin each new journey with God's purpose engrained in the intent for which the journey was designed, He provides peace so that we know that we are walking in the right direction under His leadership.

When you don't think you have the strength, when you don't think you are enough, when you think you are done, finished, and have no more to give; that's when God can use you the most. Your dependence is not on your own abilities, but in God's grace. This is when all of God meets all of you, and what seemed impossible becomes possible. His resolute grace is an uncommon grace in our lives that brings uncommon results and sustains us through every situation. We are to be strong and unmovable in our resolute decision to follow God and His ways. God's uncommon grace makes a way when there seems to be no way, and God's Word provides a strategic road map to be world changers to those who desperately need His resolute grace.

Dig a Little Deeper

1. Why is it important to live our lives with resolute clarity and resolute grace?

_____

_____

_____

2. May our passion overcome our fears to radically pursue God and His ways. What fears have you had to overcome, and how did you overcome those fears?

_____

_____

_____

3. What is the purpose in declaring dangerous declarations?

_____

_____

_____

Daily Prayer

May our daily prayer be, Lord, fill us with more of You that You might draw others to You through our lives. Help us to see You in all things, even small beginnings, and trust that You will lead us on the paths that direct our purpose. Lord, bring clarity, tenacity, and resolute grace. Let our resolve be steadfast and sure. May our lives continue to be filled with Your uncommon grace that brings uncommon results. Lord, we need You now more than ever to give us the strength and perseverance to be resolute in our walk of grace with You. Sometimes we feel overwhelmed with the pressures of this world. Make us strong and courageous. Fill us every day with Your presence and power to follow Your ways and to share You with others. Amen.

"But by the grace of God, I am what I am and His grace which was bestowed upon me was not in vain, but I labored more abundantly than they all: yet not I, but the grace of God which was with me" (1 Cor. 15:10, KJV).

"For it is by grace you have been saved, through faith—and this is not from yourselves, it is the gift of God—not by works, so that no one can boast" (Eph. 2:8–9, NIV).

DAY 2

Sustaining Grace

TWO YEARS AFTER the birth of our oldest son, Jonathan, I was diagnosed with endometriosis. I was in pain that progressively became worse and lasted five years. I went through multiple procedures, surgeries, and medications, along with the side effects; but found no relief from the pain. God sustained me with His Word and His promise of healing. My husband and I stood firm on God's Word for my healing during the waiting. I was teaching in New York during this time. During one of those years, I walked up three flights of stairs to my classroom. I was in excruciating pain. God's sustaining grace made a way each day. In the middle of many nights, I would take hot baths, sobbing with pain. My sweet husband would sit on the floor next to the tub and pray for me. His prayers brought life and sustaining grace to me. When I think of this time, I know that it was only by God's sustaining grace that we were able to make it through.

Then we were told by the doctors that I needed a hysterectomy and that we would not be able to have any more children. We were devastated. Joe and I went to church the following Sunday and at the end of the service we went to the altar. We told our pastors what the doctors had said. Our pastors and church prayed for us, for my healing and for the baby. Their faith was sustaining grace in the moment we needed it the most.

Two months later, I went to the doctor and was told I was pregnant with our second son, Matthew. He was our miracle baby. What we had been told was impossible, God had made possible. This was once again His uncommon grace for an uncommon life. God had sustained us through the pain, through the tears, through the devastating news; and in the end, God showed himself to be mighty and powerful in our lives. During the pregnancy, my healing began, and within months, there was no more pain.

Through this baby, God brought my healing. God provided an uncommon grace for an uncommon life.

My purpose in sharing this story with you is to encourage you and ensure you that what you are experiencing is truly a part of God's grace for you. Stand firm in this grace. You can count on God's sustaining grace. Sustaining grace gives you the power to keep going when you are not able to do so in your own strength. When we find ourselves at the end of ourselves, we find His grace. Peter writes to the church in I Peter to encourage them during their difficulties and "testifying that this is the true grace of God. Stand fast in it" (see 1 Pet. 5:12, NIV). Peter encouraged them by saying, "Grace and peace be yours in abundance" (1 Pet. 1:2, NIV).

God sustains us with His grace. God's grace is water in the desert. Think of a time when you were hot and thirsty, and all you could think of was getting that cool glass of water to quench your thirst. Or maybe you were like me, needing healing, needing someone to believe with you for the impossible. The Psalmist describes this time of wanting with these words: "O God, you are my God, earnestly I seek you; my soul thirsts for You, my flesh faints for You, in a dry (parched place) and weary land where there is no water" (Ps. 63:1, ESV). Our hearts are to be desperate for God to sustain us in our times of trouble. But we know that if we seek Him, He will sustain us by His grace.

David talked about this sustaining grace in Psalm 42: "As the deer pants for streams of water, so my soul pants for You Oh God. My soul thirsts for God, for the living God. When can I go and meet with God?" (Ps. 42:1-2, NIV). We cry out to God in times of trouble. We seek Him with great intensity when we need Him to intervene. Oh, how He desires that our hearts would always burn for Him!

I love this next scripture as David describes how our outstretched hands are calling to God to meet our needs. I see this as a picture of worship, longing for God and lifting our hands to Him. David says, "I spread my hands to You; my soul thirsts for You like a parched land" (Ps. 143:6, NIV). And then David goes on to say, "For with You is the fountain of life; in Your light do we see light" (Ps. 36:9, ESV). God is a fountain of forgiveness and a well spring of life. He is living water that sustains us.

Have you ever been in a dry place? Have you ever been in a place where you found yourself at the end of yourself? Have you been in a place that has brought you to your knees and you knew that only God, the Way Maker, could make a way for you? In In Isaiah 42, Isaiah is singing a song of praise to the Lord, and in this song, we see how our God has promised to make a way for us, sustaining us with His grace. "I will lead the blind by ways they have not known, along unfamiliar paths I will guide them; I will turn the darkness into light before them and make the rough places smooth. These are the things I will do; I will not forsake them" (Isa. 42:16, NIV). I love how in this scripture God promises that He will not forsake us. He will sustain us through every difficult, rough, hard place, as we hold on to hope.

God had promised Abraham many sons. But this promise had not come to pass. God's promise was realized for Abraham and Sarah when Isaac was born to them. Sarah represents grace (see Gen. 21, NKJV). Sarah had Hagar, Abraham's bondwoman, sent away into the desert. Sarah was the chosen one, the one who had favor with Abraham and with God. Hagar, representing the law, was rejected, not preferred, and cast out. Hagar was alone and had nothing to live for except her son, Ishmael. God heard her cries. During her time in the desert, God made provision for her, even though she represented the law. God sustained her for that season, providing a fountain (well) in the desert. However, Sarah had the blessing, the favor, the prosperity, and even the fulfillment of God's promise and His sustaining grace during her time of waiting for her Isaac. Sarah's Isaac was the promise fulfilled.

The desert is an empty place where you are alone and where there is little life. The scorching heat from the sun is constant. The air is so dry you can hardly breathe. You are thirsty, exhausted, and see only death around you. Your feet burn from the hot sand beneath them. There is nowhere to go, nowhere to hide or take refuge. You cannot survive the desert without God's sustaining grace. It is through this desert experience that God builds a confident faith in Him as your source and sole provider.

You may be in a desert place like Sarah, waiting for your promise, but you can be confident that God has a plan to sustain you. No matter the dark times or seasons in your life, God will not abandon you. In His grace, God holds out His hands, offering a way of escape. Grace upon grace always sustains us, inspires, and empowers us. God's uncommon grace makes a way for an uncommon life even in the middle of what seems impossible. God made a way for Sarah, and He will make a way for you as you keep your eyes focused on Him and place your life in His hands. As you rest in God's sustaining grace, He is bringing a turnaround in your situation.

Dig a Little Deeper

1. Jesus is the Way Maker. Think of a time when you had come to the end of yourself, and God made a way for you.

_____

_____

_____

2. Have you ever been in a situation when others were receiving favor and you felt that you were being treated unfairly? How did God help you in the middle of that situation?

_____

_____

_____

3. Have you experienced a desert time in your life when you were alone and unsure if God was there with you? How did God make provision for you?

_____

_____

_____

Daily Prayer

May our daily prayer be, Father, give us sustaining grace that we will dwell in Your tabernacle (draw close and worship God) and drink of Your living water. May You, Lord, refresh our souls as we thirst for You. Hear our prayer and listen to the cries of our hearts as we surrender all to You. Lord, we need your sustaining grace to see us through the daily challenges of life. Lord, help us to stay focused on You and Your assignment on our lives to carry Jesus to our world. "I pray that out of His glorious riches He may strengthen us with power through His spirit in our inner being" (Eph. 3:15). We are thankful for how You have sustained us. Amen.

"And the God of all grace, who called you to His eternal glory in Christ, after you have suffered a little while, will Himself restore you and make you strong, firm and steadfast" (1 Pet. 5:10, NIV).

"Let us therefore come boldly unto the throne of grace, that we may obtain mercy, and find grace to help in time of need" (Heb. 4:16, KJV).

DAY 3

Glory and Grace

WHILE IN HUNGARY, our mission team visited what had been an underground church during Soviet rule. They had put their lives in jeopardy each time they had met together. There was a man with a guitar that had only three strings, and that was the only instrument. Something wonderfully marvelous happened when he made the first strum on that guitar; the presence of the Lord, in all His glory, filled the room like nothing I or anyone on the team had ever experienced. Tears were rolling down our cheeks as we attempted to sing along with them. We were overwhelmed by the love of God in that place. These people had little physically. They were humble, and they knew what it was to risk their lives to meet. God honored their sacrifice, and His presence moved us, changed us, and was an experience we will never forget. God reminds me at times of these precious people and the importance to never take worship for granted and to always expect the presence of God and His glory to come when you come ready to worship Him.

> *"Turn your eyes upon Jesus. Look full in His wonderful face. And the things of earth will grow strangely dim in the light of His glory and grace."*[1]

God loves us unconditionally. He wants us to know Him in all His glory and grace. Through Christ alone can we be cleansed of our sins through His uncommon grace. Through repentance and receiving His forgiveness a way is made for us to be made whole and to be able to stand in His presence. When God looks at us, He sees us through the blood that was shed by His Son. The sacrifice that was made for us through Jesus Christ giving His life on the cross opened the way for us to be able to enter the presence of our heavenly Father. Jesus traded a crown of gold for a crown of thorns, a robe of majesty for nakedness and shame, life for death. The Psalmist declared, "O Lord, Our Lord, how majestic is Your name in all the earth! You have set Your glory above the heavens" (Ps. 8:1, ESV). God in all His glory gave His Son Jesus to provide grace to humanity.

God's glory is the essence of who He is in all His majesty. His presence is full of power and glory. We are to seek after Him, to know Him, asking Him to show us His glory. This keeps us hungering for Him and His presence. Do you have a need in your life that you have been struggling with to find the answer? When we are in God's presence, we have vision, and we behold His splendor and glory.

In David's psalm, he said, "I have seen You in the sanctuary and beheld Your power and Your glory" (Ps. 63:2, NIV). Moses had to cover his face because the glory shone so brightly from being in the presence of God (see Exod. 34:29–35, NIV). When we are in His presence, we are compelled to worship Him. David wrote in a psalm when he was in the desert of Judah, "I will praise You as long as I live, and in Your name, I will lift up my hands" (Ps. 63:4, NIV). We can worship God anywhere, in the desert or on a mountaintop. When we worship Him, we can enter into His glory. It is the gift of grace that sustains us and makes us strong and courageous to overcome darkness and live in His illuminating light.

I was in South Korea in one of the prayer grottos on Prayer Mountain. Many from throughout the world had prayed in these little rooms. Some stayed for days or weeks, fasting and praying, sleeping in the church or little rooms. As I knelt to pray, I could picture Billy Graham on his knees, Pastor Cho, and missionaries from throughout the world. I could hear prayers coming from the other rooms. They were in different languages from different countries, yet there was a mighty unity as we all prayed together. The presence of God filled those little rooms. Prayers were going up to God our Father, and He was listening. It was the first time I realized how powerfully our prayers move God and that He is listening for those who are sincere and crying out to Him. *"Winners of souls must first be weepers for souls."*[2] I discovered prayer is a prerequisite to God's presence, glory and revival.

Worship is the key that opens the door to God's glory. His glory is splendor, strength, and power. As the scriptures tell us:

"To him who is able to keep you from falling and to present you before His glorious presence without fault and with great joy—to the only God our Savior be glory, majesty, power, and authority, through Jesus Christ our Lord, before all ages, now and forevermore! Amen" (Jude 24, NIV). Worship is the gateway to God's presence and experiencing His glory.

"His glory, His presence, is found in praise. There is a shifting in your direction and a breaking of favor as you praise. He has set His glory, His presence, above the heavens. When we enter in to praise, we enter in to a heavenly, holy place. Evil cannot dwell and has no authority in God's presence."[3]

God's glory and grace brings us to a place of humility, where we see and understand that all that is not of God is wicked and in need of being burned up. We cry out for God to show us His glory. His glory brings change in us. To see His glory requires clean hands and a pure heart. We must be willing to have the hot coal to touch our lips and have God's fire to purify us. We know that worship brings us into God's presence. But to see His glory requires a life that is laid down on the altar to be cleansed and to take a posture of humility. We are to be sanctified. It is a process of being holy and set apart. As we have seen in (Isa. 6:1–6, ESV), we are to be the temples of God where His glory dwells.

"May we become the eternal dwelling place of God and soar in our ultimate assignments to be one who hosts the presence of the King of Glory. It is the unmerited favor, grace, that brings His enabling presence."[4]

God made His son as a man, yet He is crowned with all kingly authority, glory, and honor as seen in I Kings. "And when the priests came out of the Holy Place, a cloud filled the house of the Lord, so that the priests could not stand to minister because of the cloud, for the glory of the Lord filled the house of the Lord" (1 Kgs. 8:10–11, ESV). I have seen His glory in corporate worship; I have also seen His glory in personal prayer time. Whether we are on our knees or in corporate worship, when we worship our Lord, as we draw close to Him, He shows us His glory and covers us in His grace.

Because of Jesus, we have received revelation of the very characteristics of God. From that moment until now God has brought us out of the darkness into the light. He places resilient hope in us and builds endurance in an unpredictable world. When we are in His presence, we are face to face with Him, and His glory is revealed in us. God has shown us great grace in order that He might use us to show forth His glory and to draw souls to Him. We are a remnant holding on steadfastly to our faith.

Dig a Little Deeper

1. How do we bring God's glory into our lives?

_____

_____

_____

2. Think of a time when you hungered for more of God, for more of His glory in your life?

_____

_____

_____

3. Can you think of a time when you were in the presence of God and experienced His overwhelming glory?

_____

_____

_____

Daily Prayer

May our prayer be that God's uncommon grace brings us into His holy place. May His presence be with us so that we might behold His glory and dwell with Him there. Lord, show us Your glory and cover us with grace. Lord, we surrender our hearts to You that we might know You in all Your glory. Change us so that we might be more like You. Burn up all that is not of You and let us be carriers of Your presence. Empower us with Your mercy and grace that we might show compassion, forgiveness, and kindness to others. Lord, let us be light and salt to the people of this world. Lord, give us ears that hear and eyes that see Your glory and grace. Hear our prayer, Oh Lord, and may we live extraordinary lives that bring an uncommon grace to those who need you. Amen.

"But he gives us more grace. That is why the scripture says: God opposes the proud but gives grace to the humble" (Jas. 4:6, NIV).

"And the Word was made flesh and dwelt among us, (and we beheld his glory, the glory of the only begotten of the Father), full of grace and truth" (John 1:14, KJV).

DAY 4

The Gift of Grace

I WAS FIVE MONTHS pregnant with our miracle baby, our second son, Matthew. We were living in New York at that time. I was driving to school with my seven-year-old son, Jonathan. The roads were covered with ice and snow. I couldn't see the line in the median of the road or where the sides of the road ended. I looked up and saw a large truck heading straight toward my car. I only had time to say one word; in that moment I cried out, "Jesus"! I swerved into the other lane and hit another car head on. The wreck included many cars and trucks. Jonathan had a broken nose that was bleeding.

However, I could not feel anything from my waist and lower body. The ambulance came and the EMTs placed me in the ambulance with my son, Jonathan. My husband, Joe, met us at the hospital. I was unable to move from my waist to my feet. After a few tests and an ultrasound, in a room filled with doctors and staff, we were told that our baby had disconnected from the placenta. The doctor said that because of the trauma the baby was beginning to spontaneously abort. The doctors strongly recommended fully aborting the baby. They said that if it came between choosing who to save the baby or me, they would choose me. I refused any procedures for taking the baby, which was met by strong disagreement from the doctors.

Joe was with our son, Jonathan, so I was left alone in the hospital room for the night. I was still unable to move. So, I prayed. My prayer was, "Lord, no matter what happens, I will trust You. No matter what happens, I will still follow You. No matter what happens, I give my life and the life of this baby to You." There are times that you cannot control the outcome. You place your hope in God, release the situation to Him, and trust in Him. Throughout the night, the staff took ultrasounds to check on the progress of the baby. Slowly throughout the night, our baby reattached to the placenta. It was a miracle. This was a gift of grace.

The same doctors came back into my room the next day and said that even though the baby had reattached to the placenta, he had been disconnected and had not received oxygen for a period of time. The doctor said that the baby was probably severely brain injured. The doctor still recommended an abortion. I refused to sign the papers and asked to be moved to another hospital against the doctor's orders. As I was in the wheelchair leaving the hospital, I began to feel some tingling in my legs and feet. All the feelings eventually returned. Again, the gift of grace was turning my situation around.

When the doctors at the new hospital saw me, they said that the temporary paralysis had helped keep the baby stable and able to reattach. The diagnosis of brain injured could only be determined after the baby was born. Four months later, on the seventh day of the seventh month, our beautiful perfect seven-pound, seven-ounce baby boy was born. He was perfect in every way. He met all milestones early and was very bright.

In Psalm 139, we see God, Our Creator, making us:

> "For You created my inmost being, You knit me together in my mother's womb. I praise You because I am fearfully and wonderfully made; Your works are wonderful; I know that full well. My frame was not hidden from You when I was made in the secret place. When I was woven together in the depths of the earth, Your eyes saw my unformed body. All the days ordained for me were written in Your book before one of them came to be" (Ps. 139:13–16, NIV).

Psalm 139 explains that God knows us better than we know ourselves. He knows our innermost thoughts. He knows us better than any human could possibly come to know us because He is our Creator. He put us together in our mother's womb. He designed us and intended for us to be unique individuals. It wasn't by chance that we were created and designed for His purpose. It is by this gift of grace that we were created. We were fearfully and wonderfully made (see Psalm 139, ESV). He knows our heart, the way we understand and perceive things. God sees us through eyes of love and an uncommon grace.

Even though He sees our weaknesses, He sees us through eyes of mercy. "The steadfast love of the Lord never ceases; His mercies never come to an end; they are new every morning; great is Your faithfulness" (Lam. 3:22–23, ESV). He writes our stories before we live them. Remember, this is not the end of the book, so get ready for the next chapter! God asks us to "search our hearts," not to judge the hearts, motives, or intentions of others. He will reveal the parts of us that need to be changed; to bring us to a place of repentance for anything within us that is not of Him. We are to open our hearts; so that He can perform heart surgery on us and remove the parts of our heart that are not functioning in love. There is a shifting and a sifting that takes place. The Psalmist cried out, "Search me, O God, and know my heart; test me and know my anxious thoughts. See if there is any offensive way in me and lead me in the way everlasting" (Ps. 139:23–24, NIV). This is my life verse.

We are to be led by Him and to walk in His ways. This is the opposite of walking in our offensive nature. When our hearts become one with His, our desires are one with God's desires for us; and we are anxious for nothing. When we ask God to search and test us, to know our thoughts, He sees every offensive way and leads us to a place of repentance that brings change. "For we are God's workmanship, created in Christ Jesus to do good works, which God prepared in advance for us to do" (Eph. 2:10, NIV).

We are a masterpiece on which He is still working. As His presence fills us and abides in us, then His character also takes residence in us. "For it is by grace you have been saved, through faith—and this is not from yourselves. It is the gift of God—not by works, so that no one can boast" (Eph. 2:8–9, NIV). You were designed to fulfill God's radical purpose for your life and the calling that ultimately leads others to Christ. "But because of His great love for us, God, who is rich in mercy, made us alive with Christ even when we were dead in transgressions—it is by the gift of grace you have been saved"

(Eph. 2:4, NIV). There is a world that is watching. Are they seeing Jesus in you? Be a gatekeeper like the Levites, living a holy life. Be holy people that live what they say and are hungry for God. We are to live on purpose, having Him at the center of our lives.

Our miracle baby is now a pediatrician, helping other little babies and children to live and thrive. The gift of grace made a way for the impossible to be possible. I have heard it said, "Faith goes into the future and pulls it into the now." Sometimes miracles come quickly, a now, immediate answer to prayer. Other times we go through a season of waiting and trusting. Both seasons require a trusting relationship with God.

Dig a Little Deeper

1. What is meant by the scriptures that we are fearfully and wonderfully made?

_____

_____

_____

2. For what purpose do you think God created you?

_____

_____

_____

3. As we abide in Christ, we take on His character. What does that do in us?

_____

_____

_____

Daily Prayer

"Search me, O God, and know my heart; test me and know my anxious thoughts. See if there is any offensive way in me and lead me in the way everlasting" (see Ps. 139, NIV). Lord, guide us and direct our paths. Keep our hearts stayed on You. Lord, establish the works of our hands (see Ps. 90:17, NIV). May our lives be a blessing to others. Lord, You know us better than we know ourselves. Lay the pieces of our lives on Your altar and burn away all that is not of You. Thank you for Your provision and blessings. You know our needs before we even ask. We praise and thank You that we have found favor with You. We are Your sons and daughters, and we are greatly blessed. Amen.

"And God is able to make all grace abound toward you; that ye, always having all sufficiency in all things, may abound to every good work" (2 Cor. 9:8, KJV).

"Therefore, as ye abound in everything in faith, and utterance, and knowledge, and in all diligence, and in your love to us, see that ye abound in this grace also" (2 Cor. 8:7, KJV).

DAY 5

Sovereign Grace

W E ARE LIVING in a time when the world is in crisis. Not only can you survive these times, but you can learn to move forward in them through sovereign grace. We are to be people of purpose. We are to live on purpose, love on purpose, and give on purpose. To be sovereign is to possess supreme power and authority. Jesus has provided sovereign grace to live in these times. "Who has saved us and called us to a holy life—not because of anything we have done but because of His own purpose and grace. This grace was given to us in Christ Jesus before the beginning of time" (2 Tim. 1:9, NIV).

God births in us His vision and plan for our lives. Then He covers us with His sovereign grace to take the gospel to the world. God's divine mission statement is: "For God so loved the world, that He gave His only Son, that whoever believes in Him should not perish but have eternal life" (John 3:16, ESV). God reminds us that "Before I formed you in the womb I knew you, before you were born, I set you apart; I appointed you a prophet to the nations" (Jer. 1:5, NIV). He gave us an uncommon grace to live an uncommon life. We need Jesus to live intentionally in these times.

My husband, Joe, and I were in Germany. The country had been flooded with refugees from Serbia, at that time. My heart burned with compassion for these people, but we had been told to be careful and to avoid possible dangerous situations involving gangs that had formed. We were in the last car on the train going from one part of Germany to another. No one was in the car with us until just as the train was beginning to start. Then five Serbian men jumped into the car with us. They had been drinking alcohol and were drinking more as they were talking loudly. They knew we were Americans

26

and began asking us questions and loudly making negative statements about our president and our country.

I took my husband's hand, and we grasped the steal bar in front of us. We closed our eyes and began to pray in the spirit. We knew these men could speak and understand some English, but they would not know what we were praying in the spirit. When we opened our eyes, they were all gone. The train had not stopped, and there was nowhere they could have gone unless they had jumped off the train while it was moving. We know that God intervened supernaturally to protect us. His sovereign grace covered us and protected us. I believe they saw Jesus in us and knew they could not touch us. God is all powerful, sovereign, and has all authority in our lives.

We are to have a burning heart for the lost and hopeless. This is the miracle of His sovereign grace. We are called out to be sent out, and He prepares us before He sends us out. "Then I heard the voice of the Lord saying, 'Whom shall I send, and who will go for Us?' And I said, 'Here I am! Send me'" (Isa. 6:8, ESV). "You were anointed and appointed for your calling before the foundation of the earth was established."[5]

It takes faith to be God-sent. Without faith, we are unable to please God. With God, all things are possible. We serve a limitless God. We are to awaken to purpose to take Jesus to a lost and dying world. There is no call more important or more fulfilling. As we have often heard said, "We live, we worship, we give, we preach, all to please One."[6] We are to run and pray together in covenant unity to do great and mighty things for the glory of God.

Jeremiah said, "Behold I am the Lord. The God of all flesh. Is anything too hard for Me?" (Jer. 32:27, ESV). We are to come before God confidently and ask anything in His name: "Call to Me and I will answer you and tell you great and hidden things that you have not known" (Jer. 33:3, ESV). You've got to want, value, and go after God in the hard places, in the process, for God and His Word to prevail over you. Your purpose and calling are not all about you, but they are always about bringing others into relationship with God.

I was nineteen, flying in a four-seater plane with two pastors and Bishop Fernando Palomo, the Bishop of the Methodist Church of Costa Rica. The Costa Rican mountains below us were breathtaking. After landing, we went to an area at the base of the mountains. There was a small house and a small building with a dirt floor that served as the church. We were there to meet with pastors and youth pastors from throughout that area of Costa Rica. Many had traveled on foot for many hours and some for days. We came the day prior to the beginning of the youth camp.

I was told that the people in the mountains all around us would begin a journey early Sunday morning and walk for hours down the mountain to get to the church service. They would stay together all day; then they would begin the journey back up the mountain. Many of the youth coming to this camp would be traveling down those mountains. They had an appointment with God that would determine their future.

I went to sleep that night on a mat on the floor and woke up as the sun was rising. I heard a sound coming from outside that I had never heard before. I got dressed and hurried outside. No one was there, but I could still hear the sound. As I walked closer to the church, the sound became louder. I slowly opened the church door and there on the dirt floor, face down in the dirt, I saw the bishop, the pastors, the youth pastors, all crying out to God. It was a heavenly sound, indescribable, a holy sound.

It was nothing I had ever heard before. I don't know if they had been there all night, but I knew their hearts were believing for God's sovereign grace to move on the hearts of these young people. Later, I asked the bishop what were they doing on the floor? He said, *"We are praying for the young people who will be coming to this camp. They will be the next generation of pastors, bishops, missionaries, and teachers. If they do not accept the call to take Jesus to the people, then there will be none to tell the next generation about Jesus."*

As I saw the youth come in, some in the back of trucks, and others walking down the mountainsides, I began to weep. I knew the importance of the decisions they would be making. And I knew the sacrifice of those godly men who had been praying for them. God moved mightily, and I saw those men wrapping their arms around the young men as they made commitments to follow Jesus and to tell others of His saving grace.

Grace is the empowering presence of God that enables us to be that person He has called us. Everyone is unique in their calling. I invite you to step into His crucifixion to be Christ-like though His sovereign grace. He makes beauty from brokenness, breaking chains of hopelessness. It is through God's sovereign, supremely powerful, and empowering presence, and grace that we live uncommon lives.

Dig a Little Deeper

1. God covers us to take His sovereign grace to the world. What is His divine mission?

   _____

   _____

   _____

2. What does it mean to have God's vision birthed in us?

   _____

   _____

   _____

3. What does it look like to you to have a burning heart for the lost and hopeless?

_____

_____

_____

Daily Prayer

Here I am, Lord, send me. May we extend compassion to a hurting world. I have decided to follow Jesus. Though none go with me, still I will follow. May our hearts burn for the lost and undone to come to know Your sovereign grace. May our hearts, minds, souls, and spirits be flooded to overflowing. Let Your love reign in our lives today. You make all things new. You bind up the broken-hearted. All that has been lost, You restore. You cover us with a banner of grace that protects us. You hold us in Your arms when we are hurting. Your sovereign grace helps us to go after You even in the hard places. May we always desire to be close to you. Amen.

"But unto every one of us is given grace according to the measure of the gift of Christ" (Eph.4:7, KJV).

"For sin shall not have dominion over you for ye are not under the law, but under grace" (Rom. 6:14, KJV).

DAY 6

Unrelenting Grace

G RACE IS AN intensely personal experience that happens at the core of the soul, where Christ meets with us one-on-one to revolutionize the way we view life. My husband, Joe, and I were infected with COVID-19 during the beginning of the virus. There were no vaccines or medications available. There were no available beds at the hospital. I sat for one day in a wheelchair in a closet area in the hospital and received some medical treatment. But there was no other help available. At the end of that day, we went home.

We stayed home for months unable to see our children or grandchildren. My husband, Joe, took care of me and himself. I struggled with an extremely high fever for many weeks. I didn't know where I was or what was happening around me. But somehow in the middle of this time, I knew God was there and that He was bigger than the virus. I had an assurance in my spirit that I would eventually come out of the virus. It took months for me to recover my strength. It was God's unrelenting grace that saw me through this time. We lost family and friends to the virus or conditions possibly associated with the virus. I can't answer why some made it through this time and recovered and others were called to heaven. I can say that God's unrelenting grace brought comfort to our broken hearts and made a way for many to go through the most difficult time in their lives. We honor and will forever miss those who began their heavenly journey during this time.

Just as I was completing recovery from COVID-19, I was diagnosed with skin cancer. I went through five procedures and three surgeries over several months. When one procedure was completed, another cancer site or tumor would be found. I became exhausted with the constant battle. The cancer journey I had been on brought me to a place of knowing the voice of

God in the middle of the storm and resting in His assurance that He would see me through. If you are feeling hopeless, exhausted, or burdened, may God's unrelenting grace take hold of your heart.

Have you seen God meet you during your struggles lately? God is intense, strong, has momentum, and is fierce. We serve an unrelenting God who provides unrelenting grace to us in these times. Jesus was on a boat in the Sea of Galilee when a storm arose. In the middle of the storm, Jesus spoke a word, "And he saith to them, 'Why are you fearful. O ye of little faith?' Then he arose and rebuked the winds and the sea; and there was a great calm" (Matt. 8:26, KJV). One word can bring peace in the middle of your situation or storm.

In the middle of the storm, we cry out: "The name of the Lord is a strong tower; the righteous run to it and are safe" (Prov. 18:10, NIV). In these times we are reminded, "For You have been my refuge, a strong tower against the foe. I long to dwell in Your tent forever and take refuge in the shelter of Your wings" (Ps. 61:3–4, NIV). We have been brought from being a sinner unclean and undone to being covered in His unrelenting grace and bought with the price of God's Son's blood. He paid the price when He purchased us with His own life. God takes us from condition to position. We are covered in grace, compassion, and a passion to see others redeemed. Jesus is our strength, our constant help in our time of need. He gives us the strength to be relentless.

Painful times cause us to refocus, get our attention, cause us to reprioritize, humble us, let us see our limitations, and cause us to trust God and His unrelenting grace. There is one thing we can all be sure of, and that is there will be change. Some change comes suddenly, and other change comes over time. There are sudden shifts that can change your life forever. When change comes, we stand fast in His unrelenting grace. Unrelenting is a "don't quit" attitude. Your answer may be coming in this next move or around the next corner. *"The word of prophecy is pregnant with what God wants to birth. You are pregnant with something heaven wants to birth."* Just as an anointed word in season brings truth, light, understanding, guidance, and shifts the atmosphere; when we depend on God for everything, our humility brings supernatural victory and a shift in our circumstance. When God changes your life, He also changes the lives of those you influence.

May we count the cost and have the mind of Christ. "For He is the kind of man who is always thinking about the cost" (Prov. 23:7, NIV). "As he thinks in his heart, so is he" (Prov. 23:7, AMP). When God changes us, we will never be the same. We change our minds to think as Christ thinks, and His unrelenting grace provides tenacity and determination. We will have different attitudes, actions, and attributes. We will be life changers. When our passion meets God's purpose, life is breathed into others. The results will look like Jesus.

Have you ever found yourself in the middle of a perilous time? What is your first response when you are looking for help to get through the situation? Do you automatically turn to Jesus? When our hearts and minds are turned to Jesus, we find the answers we are seeking. However, there are times the answer we thought we would get from God is different from the one we receive. The Lord of the harvest is the Lord of the outcome. It takes faith to propel, not fear that paralyzes. Discover God's purpose for your life and live out God's call on your life intentionally. When you yield yourself to the Lord, a shifting takes place in every part of you. You overcome fear to walk out God's plan in your life with faith. Anything worth doing will come at a cost.

Change your mind. Change your heart. Change your life. Change others. Change can come unexpectedly, and it can come by choice. Difficult situations don't build character; they reveal it. In the middle of the situation, who you are, your character, is revealed. As the Psalmist said, "Wherever I go, Your hand will guide me; Your strength will empower me. It is impossible to disappear from You or to ask the darkness to hide me, for Your presence is everywhere, bringing light into my night" (Ps. 139:10–11, TPT). He is the God of the outcome.

God calls us and gives us an assignment. He puts his message within us, then He anoints us, puts His mantle on us, and equips us to carry out the assignment. Be brave, strong, hopeful, and joyful as you receive God's grace in your life. Then you can walk out that assignment with unrelenting grace.

Be intentional and strategic as you fulfill your assignment staying focused on Jesus. So, stand strong and give thanks to the God who made you, trains you, and empowers you to live a life with unrelenting grace.

Dig a Little Deeper

1. Grace is an intensely personal experience that happens at the core of the soul, where Christ meets with us one-on-one to revolutionize the way we view life. When you have applied grace to your life, how has God revolutionized your life or your view of life?

    _____

    _____

    _____

2. Have you been through a difficult time, yet in the middle of the struggle, you could hear God directing you? How has this impacted your life?

    _____

    _____

    _____

3. Can you think of a time when you had prayed and expected a specific answer, only to get a different answer from God? Has He ever surprised you? God is a mystery, and He so graciously reveals Himself to us.

_____

_____

_____

Daily Prayer

May our daily prayer be that we run to You, Lord, as our Protector and Source of strength in our time of need and that we will hold fast to Your unrelenting grace. We dwell in Your presence and rest in Your peace. You equip and empower us to follow You. We trust You, Lord, and we will always serve You. Lord, let us make a difference in the lives of others. May our "Jesus Walk" have a positive influence on those You place in our lives. Make us to be faithful and steadfast. In the times of difficulty, we hold fast to You and Your unrelenting grace. As we live this life that often seems so ordinary, let us live extraordinary lives with unrelenting grace. Amen.

"Moreover, the law entered, that the offence might abound. But where sin abounded grace did much more abound: That as sin hath reigned unto death, even so might grace reign through righteousness unto eternal life by Christ our Lord" (Rom. 5:20–21, KJV).

"Grace and peace be multiplied unto you through the knowledge of God, and of Jesus our Lord" (2 Pet. 1:2, KJV).

DAY 7

A Touch of Grace

G OD'S LOVE IS revealed in your compassion toward others. It only takes a touch of grace to change a life. God provides restoration of a broken heart. When you forgive, the chains are broken off, then you are free to be chain breakers and crown restorers for others.

My granddaughter, Everly, loves to dance in her beautiful, twirly dresses and ballet outfits. And, of course, she loves wearing her tiara. She loves to worship as she dances. However, Everly in her short, six-year-old life has had to overcome fears and anxiety. She has learned that God is with her and that He is helping her to be successful in every endeavor. She was having trouble sleeping in her new bedroom alone. But her mom and dad prayed with her, read the Bible with her, and every night she goes to sleep with the song: "Way Maker." The other day, she called me to come close, and she whispered in my ear, "I asked Jesus in my heart." Everly not only came to know Jesus as her Savior, but she also learned to be fearless. Just a touch of grace takes away our fears and anxiety and makes us strong and fearless.

"Heavenly Father daily restores crowns to the fallen and hurting, the forgotten and those who feel they least deserve it by restoring dignity and honor. We are to be Royal Crown Restorers as daughters of the King."[8] The crown represents authority, honor, position, and glory. It represents the splendor of His Majesty. You are a citizen of the kingdom. The kingdom mindset is faith, a God kind of faith, which is your rightful inheritance. Expect kingdom results because you are agents of the kingdom and with the kingdom citizenship comes rights. A kingdom mindset says you look to the King for confirmation. He places in you a confident humility enabling you to serve Him.

When I was in college, I had a roommate who had only been a Christian a few months when we first met. She was so excited about her relationship with Jesus, and she loved learning about Him. She pursued Him with all her heart. We prayed together and studied the Bible together. She was in church or Bible study every time there was opportunity. She has continued to pursue God and has been a youth pastor, as well as serving in other areas of the church. Her tender heart toward God caused her to be easily convicted.

One day I came into the dorm and found her boxing up many of her clothes. She was taking them to Goodwill. When I asked her why; she said that she had shoplifted clothes before she came to know Jesus, and she was convicted and couldn't wear them anymore. Her tender heart kept her moving forward and growing in God. She had been rescued by Jesus and set on a new path. Jesus had restored her crown, and she was a light to all who knew her. Just a touch of grace can bring conviction and restoration.

> *"Twas grace that taught my heart to fear, and grace my fears relieved, how precious did that grace appear the hour I first believed."*⁹

Let your pain become your inspiration, turning your pain into purpose. His presence is in the middle of your cries. Diamonds are made from the pressure applied while in the earth. You are jewels in His crown, diamonds of purpose. God's grace is unconditional. His grace is undeniably, overwhelmingly, never-ending, always pressing, pushing you forward, and never retreating. You are to have a mind perspective that says you desire to advance, even when there is a counterattack. In the natural, you may see failure, lack of movement forward, never seeing your destiny fulfilled. Don't be surprised when things don't seem to go your way; rejection is for redirection. With just a touch of grace, God gives perspective to make it through your darkest night. You are sitting on your destiny if you are not putting forth the effort to move forward. God is calling you to restore crowns in your world.

What are you doing with your giftings? In the Bible, we see those who, when they didn't get to do what they set out to do, ended up where they needed to be to accomplish what God had set out for them to do. God was moving them in position for His blessings. Sometimes even bad things can lead to good things. Everything in your life is of purpose for your growth in grace. Some brokenness comes from things that happen that are not of your own making, while other brokenness comes from choices, sometimes bad choices you have made. A touch of grace brings you back to the heart of the Father.

The scriptures tell us, "For it is by grace you have been saved, through faith and this is not from yourselves, it is the gift of God" (Eph. 2:8, NIV). You are His workmanship to do good works. You are to be in God's order and plan. People are waiting on you to help them to find their way, and you can only help them in your unique way. God only demands of you your own uniqueness. It just takes a touch of grace to be strong in faith, love, and belief. You are complete in God. Everything you need is inside of you. You are to be authentic, unpredictable, unusual, and faithful.

I have heard it said, *Jonathan Edwards in the Great Awakening (1734–1749) said that we are to die daily to the flesh to bring revival to the hearts of mankind.* In the first great wakening (1720s–1740s), there was an emphasis on grace. You are to have an intense fire power within you that purifies you and transforms others. You are to call forth the kingdom in others to bring breakthrough in their lives. The scriptures tell us, "So He said to me, 'This is the word of the Lord to Zerubbabel: Not by might nor by power, but by my Spirit, says the Lord Almighty'" (see Zech. 4:6, NIV). God does not require anything too great, but He does require you to choose Him over your fears, hurts, and strongholds. With His grace, He provides all we will need to follow Him.

The enemy only attempts to attack you to distract you from your assignment. Your assignment is your calling, your purpose, your destiny; your life's legacy, and His anointing to change the world. You are to change your world and to say "yes" to His call on your life; then you will find others and help them to find the Savior so they can be touched by His grace.

I once heard Daniel Fusco, Lead Pastor Crossroads Community Church in Vancouver, WA. say, *"God has a plan for your life. Don't be consumed by situations. Keep your eyes fixed on Jesus. Faith cures the troubled heart. We must have unstoppable hope. We are to live above the circumstances. We can find faith in uncertain times. Exercise the faith God has given you in these troubling times. Faith is a choice we get to exercise. He is an amazingly good*

Father. Look at everything in the context of eternity. Jesus' return is eminent. We follow Jesus because He is the way, the truth, the life."[10]

Dig a Little Deeper

1. How does forgiveness impact your ability to serve the Lord and love others?

   _____

   _____

   _____

2. Think of a time that you were convicted and your life was changed.

   _____

   _____

   _____

3. Can you think of a time in your life when God's presence was in the middle of your cries?

   _____

   _____

   _____

Daily Prayer

Let our daily prayer be that our need for You, O God, is greater than our fears. Let our prayer be that we will become more like our Savior through serving others; willing to make sacrifices; and be royal crown restorers. May we daily make an appointment with You for Bible study and prayer, spending time in Your presence and leaning in to hear Your voice. May we keep in mind it only takes a touch of Your grace to change lives. May we live a life of forgiveness and humility, putting others' needs above our own.

Thank you for empowering us, especially in times when we are afraid to keep going. May our lives touch others with Your grace. Amen.

"And if by grace, then it is no longer by works: if it were, grace would no longer be grace" (Rom. 11:6, NIV).

"The Lord is merciful and gracious, slow to anger, and plenteous in mercy" (Ps. 103:8, KJV).

DAY 8

Radical Grace

WHEN OUR YOUNGEST child, our miracle baby, was only a day old, we were told that he had a heart murmur and that a heart valve was closed. I thought, "How could this be? He is our miracle baby!" We were told that he would need a few days to grow a little stronger, then they would need to do surgery on his heart. We took our baby home. We had a choice to believe God for another miracle or to live in fear that he would not survive the surgery. We began to radically pray and cry out to God for a miracle. We knew it would take radical grace to make our child whole.

We went to Buffalo Children's Hospital, and we met with the top pediatric cardiac surgeon. As the medical team were running tests, we sat in a waiting area with parents waiting to see the surgeon for their babies and children. My heart broke for all those in that room, knowing they were all praying for a miracle just like we were. We were called to go into a room to wait for the surgeon, but instead a nurse came in and said that they needed to run the tests a second time. We waited and we prayed with a radical trust for the impossible.

The surgeon came in to talk with us. He stumbled over his words as he began to say, "I don't know if you are people of faith, but there are times when God chooses to reach down from heaven and create a miracle that I cannot explain as a surgeon. I don't know why God chose your child, but He did. Matthew's heart is completely healthy. There is no heart murmur, and the valve to the heart is open. The only way I can explain this is that God has done a miracle." We were overwhelmed by the radical grace God had extended to our child and our family.

As we left the surgeon's office and walked past the waiting room with all the other parents waiting anxiously with hope for their own children; my heart fell to my stomach, knowing our child was now miraculously whole, but some of them would be going through great struggles and possible heartaches. My spirit began to pray radically on their behalf trusting God and His grace, placing those babies in His hands.

"Miracles are supernatural interventions in the natural affairs of man."[11] *"God is faithful. Be relentless in your pursuit of Him. On the other side of your obedience is your miracle."*[12] Radical grace is being relentless in your pursuit of God and faithfully believing in Him for your miracle. *"God does nothing on earth without our prayers."*[13]

Jacob was the third generation of Abraham. He was a miracle baby with purpose. Jacob loved Rachel, and he was willing to work twice the time to make Rachel his wife. Jacob wrestled the angel for his blessing, but his wrestling left him with a limp—a reminder that God had changed him. "For you have struggled with God and man" (see Gen. 32:28, NIV). Have you wrestled with God? Have you ever found yourself getting radical with God to bring about your miracle?

When you want something you have never had before, you must do something you have never done before. This takes radical grace in your life. As we seek after God, we must be willing to be radically changed from the inside out. An encounter with Jesus will change you. Like Moses, choose to go into God's presence. Moses went to the mountaintop to lean in closer to God. Go before your heavenly Father and fellowship with Him. Turn your heart to Him, seek Him, hear Him, then you will find Him. Pray and never give up (see Luke 18:1, NIV). Have shameless persistence (see Luke 11:9, NIV). Choose as Moses did to have a heart of prayer.

God's radical grace propels us to go after God with all our hearts. We are to have an accountable tenacity, with open minds and strong, brave hearts. We are to be courageous and chase after God. Success can be sudden, quick, and happen overnight. However, the smallest amount of energy, exceedingly small increments, baby steps, can be part of your process in following God and His plan for your life. You are to walk in intense faith. God gives us all we need. Persevere with tenacity and boldness. Hold on when you feel like quitting. Don't despise small beginnings; the Lord rejoices for the work to begin (see Zech. 4:10, NIV).

There is a season to plant, a season to harvest, and a time to rest. There is a season for watering, nurturing, and trimming back (see Ecclesiastes 3:2, NIV). Know the season you are currently in. Find purpose in it. Celebrate accomplishments on purpose. Give God credit for what He has done. Stay focused and accountable. Be willing to let go of one thing to grab hold of another thing.

Be challenged in your vision and see the vision clearly. God will not be late on the appointed day. Run with the vision, and you will not grow weary if you stay focused. Run aggressively toward the vision with intensity. Have a Joshua spirit in the Valley of Decision to take the land. Complete God's assignment on your life. God qualifies the called. Run courageously toward God, and let his radical grace empower you to serve in radical excellence. Times of prayer prepare us to go forth.

Pastor Jack Hayford said, *"Prayer is invading the impossible."*[14] Simply believe the Word of God, and He will show up. Prime your prayer like priming a water pump. As Jesus said, "So, I say to you: 'Ask and it shall be given to you; seek and you will find; knock and the door will be opened to you'" (Luke 11:9, NIV). Ask and keep on asking, seek and keep on seeking, knock and keep on knocking. God gives us a voice to cry out boldly to Him. He raises the volume of our voices to cry out for the world.

We are to shamelessly and radically come before God and abandon protocol to get what is needed. We are to ceaselessly petition God and trust in His radical grace. It is the Father's good pleasure to give good things. He is available anytime and in any circumstance. Your assignment is to ask; His commitment is to give you as much as you need. Jeremiah says it so perfectly: "Call to me and I will answer you and tell you great and unsearchable things you do not know" (Jer. 33:3, NIV). Ask with shameless boldness and audacity. God wants to heal and restore you, empower and give you all you need. Run the course. Finish what God has started.

We are to be in personal pursuit of the Lord. *"Do you know Jesus as intimate liquid love from the Father? Knowing this Good News, you can't help but share it."*[15]

Dig a Little Deeper

1. Do you have a radical trust for the impossible? Can you think of a time when you had to step out into a radical trust for God?

_____

_____

_____

2. Radical grace propels us to go after God with all our hearts. What does radical grace mean to you?

_____

_____

_____

3. Is there a time in your life that you have struggled to trust God? How did you find your faith in God in that situation?

_____

_____

_____

Daily Prayer

Father may our prayer be that our heart's focus will always be turned toward our Savior. May we always desperately seek after You and be in relationship with You. May we shamelessly and boldly pursue You. Lord, help me to be salt and light in the world. Let everything we do be for Your glory and honor, Lord. We radically cry out to You to fill us with Your presence so that we can fulfill our life's calling and assignment. Help us to persevere with tenacity in our walk with You. Lord, change us from the inside out to have the integrity and power to fulfill the call on our lives. Lord, give us the strength to run with vision and stay focused. Never allow us to be so consumed by our emotions that we lose sight of You and Your love for us. Lord, give us eyes that see, ears that hear and hearts that understand. Let our prayers arise like incense. May we seek the Miracle Worker more than the miracle. Amen.

"What shall we say then? Shall we continue in sin, that grace may abound? God forbid. How shall we say, we that are dead to sin, live any longer therein? Know ye not that so many of us were baptized into Jesus Christ were baptized into his death?" (Rom. 6:1–3, KJV).

"He which testifies these things saith, Surely, I come quicky. Amen. Even so, come, Lord Jesus. The grace of our Lord Jesus Christ be with you all. Amen" (Rev. 22:20–21, KJV).

DAY 9

Empowering Grace

During a mission outreach in Budapest, Hungary, we set up in the middle of a park area that was surrounded by multi-level apartment buildings. These buildings had been used to hide Jews during the war. There was a sense of God's presence in that place. We laid out tarps on the ground and cranked up the music. Soon the tarps were covered with children, and adults stood around the back of the children. We began to minister in English through an interpreter. We worshiped, danced, had object lessons, and played games with the children. We shared Jesus with them and how they could come to know Him as their Savior.

We looked up, and all around us, the apartment windows opened, and families, young and old, were looking down on us and hearing the Gospel being shared with them. Many raised their hands to ask Jesus in their hearts and lives. We had come just to minister to a few children, but God with His empowering grace opened the hearts of these people living where God's children had once been hidden from the enemy. God empowered us to share the Gospel, and by His grace, many came to know the Lord that day.

Jesus, by his death and resurrection made a declaration of a revolution through His empowering grace. Rallying the church around a common cause and a commitment of living a life declaring Jesus Christ as Lord is a radical and empowering declaration that changes lives and the world of those who will believe. These declarations change the culture and the atmosphere. God's empowering grace closes the doors to old things and opens doors to God-given opportunities.

One of my favorite places in Israel is the Western Wall. Seeing all the thousands of little pieces of paper with prayers written on them placed between the stones was powerful! So many people were crying out to God and believing on behalf of so many others was such an example of God's empowering grace. As we prayed, we were empowered with faith and revelation of God's grace for those we prayed.

The Word of God empowers us through revelation, which is insight in God's truth for edification, enlightenment, and equipping of the saints. We are equipped and empowered by God to lead and to serve. We are to be established in Him. Empowering grace is unconditional and exceeds the limits of what is common and ordinary. Making bold, dangerous declarations brings empowerment. At Jesus's birth, He brought an empowering declaration that threatened Herod, causing him to come against Him (see Luke 2:13–14, NIV). An empowering declaration will bring peace, rally people around a common cause, and is powerful. We are empowered to live a victorious life through His grace.

A revolutionary declaration was exclaimed to the world by the disciples as they encountered Jesus and laid down their lives, turning their world upside down. Isaiah gives us a picture of these common men living uncommon lives. "Behold the former things have come to pass, and new things I now declare; before they spring forth, I tell you of them" (Isa. 42:9, ESV). "Return to the stronghold, you prisoners of hope. Even today I declare that I will restore double to you" (Zech. 9:12, NKJV). We are to make an empowering declaration of the unusual, exceptional, and supernatural. Ezekiel brought life into what was not alive. His words brought life, making dead bones come to life. God wants to permeate your life so that you are used in your harvest field of influence. He wants to turn your world upside down just as He did in Acts (see Acts 17:5–6, ESV).

An empowering declaration was made boldly by John the Baptist, declaring the arrival of Jesus. An empowering declaration should bring change. Jesus's life was full of powerful declarations of healing, supernaturally raising the dead, turning water into wine, and walking on the water. From the cross, He made the greatest declaration. Through His life and in His death and resurrection, He declared salvation to a lost world. This empowering declaration made by Paul and Silas of the Gospel and His empowering grace turned the disciples' world upside down, as they were told to lay down their lives.

We should be a clear and present danger to the enemy. The enemy should be running when he sees you coming. You are to be armed and dangerous. A dangerous declaration is revolutionary. An empowering declaration with a revolutionary purpose and plan of the almighty God was exclaimed through Jesus when He declared the beatitudes and when He declared, "You are the salt of the earth, but if salt has lost its taste, how shall its saltiness be restored? You are the light of the world. A city set on a hill cannot be hidden" (see Matt. 5:13–14, ESV).

An empowering declaration should be contagious. Everyone who meets you, should be changed by Jesus in you; they should see in you something they want in their lives. Know the wisdom of what God is saying and apply it. Proverbs tell us, "I guide you in the way of wisdom and lead you along straight paths" (Prov. 4:11, NIV). The Holy Spirit is your guide and teacher. He leads you along straight paths. He promises to be with you. He makes the crooked paths straight. He will lead and guide you with the truth.

Live a life of forgiveness that empowers you to restore others. "Jesus answered, 'I am the way and the truth and the life. No one comes to the Father except through me" (John 14:6, NIV). God's empowering grace leads us in the way.

Pray and fast to get the mind of God. "But Thou, O Lord, art a shield for me; my glory, and the lifter of mine head" (Ps. 3:3, KJV). Connect His power to your strength. Be transformed into His image. Be witnesses to your world (see Acts 1:8, NIV). You are a light bearer. Don't just do a little; but give God your best (see Matt. 6:22, NIV). Empowering grace enables us to have a burning and longing heart for God. Purification through baptism with fire purifies us and prepares us for the Bridegroom, Jesus the Messiah. The Lord wants to brand our hearts with His fire. Our cry should be, "Oh Lord, come quickly." We should be longing for the Bridegroom to come. As the Church, we are the bride of Christ. We should be about our Father's business, carrying the Gospel to the world and preparing ourselves as the bride for the Bridegroom. There must be a burning and longing, for the

Bridegroom is coming soon. He is to be the most important one in our lives. He empowers us to live in His grace, love Him, and show compassion to a world that desperately needs Him.

Dig a Little Deeper

1. Give an example of an empowering declaration.

    _____

    _____

    _____

2. Give an example of empowering grace in your life.

    _____

    _____

    _____

3. The Word of God empowers us through revelation. Give an example from the scriptures of empowering revelation.

    _____

    _____

    _____

Daily Prayer

Lord, may we daily declare Your Word to this world and bring life to the lost. Lord, empower us to live every moment in the light of Your ways. May we be empowered by Your grace. Lord, You, are everything we desire. You are our hearts cry. You breathe life into the lost and change hearts. May our lives impact others. Help us to keep our eyes on You and off our own struggles. Lord, may we seek to meet the needs of others. There is a burning and longing in our hearts for You to return. Lord, take over our hearts and emotions. Let our lives shine as we go after You wholeheartedly. May we walk the walk of the Spirit and the walk of power as we walk with You, Jesus. Amen.

"That being justified by His grace, we should be made heirs according to the hope of eternal life" (Titus 3:7, KJV).

"In whom we have redemption through His blood. The forgiveness of sins, according to the riches of His grace" (Eph. 1:7, KJV).

DAY 10

Forgiving Grace

UNFORGIVENESS IS FERTILE soil for instability. Decisions made in a moment of anger are often bad decisions. Words spoken out of hurt are often hurtful. Hurting people often hurt others. Before you can give, you must forgive. This weight that so easily besets us impacts marriages, self-image, avoidance of truth, and is a hinderance to serving. It does not matter if you are right or if you have been treated unfairly or unjustly. It does not matter what someone else says, perceives, or how you were wronged. You determine your response to the situation. Have you ever dealt with a spirit of unforgiveness?

At one time, my husband and I were children's ministry leaders. One Sunday, two of the six-year-old girls began fighting. It was not a pretty sight. They were slapping, pushing, pulling hair, and literally on the floor rolling around before we could pull them apart. There were hair and bows flying everywhere. Now both young ladies were strong-willed and have strong personalities. One of the girls was quick to compose herself and offered a heartfelt apology. I was not surprised, as I knew she was strong-willed, but also very tenderhearted. The other girl was asked if she was ready to forgive but replied a very defiant, "No!" She went on to say that she needed some time to think about it. We were surprised by her response. After all, we couldn't make her forgive or accept the other girl's apology. We prayed with the girls and before the end of the class, both girls had somewhat reluctantly apologized and had forgiven each other. This experience changed my perception of forgiveness. Yes, we are to forgive, and yes, we are to seek the forgiveness of others we have hurt. However, we may need some time for God to work it out in our hearts. Forgiveness is often a process.

Through His blood poured out for us at Calvary, we find forgiveness; and through His unfailing love, we extend forgiveness to others. Forgiveness is a key element to entering His presence and experiencing His glory. Without forgiveness extended to others, we have hearts that are unable to enter God's forgiving grace. We must forgive because we have been forgiven so much! Forgiveness is a God-shifting moment. Forgiveness embraces grace. There is a forever forgiveness that lasts for a lifetime. Forgiveness empowers you to restore others, even when natural fears and insecurities hold you back. Stop listening to the voices in your head and listen to the one voice that brings you freedom. Forgiveness is a choice and a change of heart.

> *"Forgiveness is not dependent on what someone else does. If you have ever been hurt, abused, misused, deceived, or disappointed; you can choose to forgive. If you are waiting for an apology, stop waiting. Decide that you will not let unforgiveness steal your joy and peace of mind. You will never be as effective for God if your heart harbors revenge. You must forgive."*[16]

With God's uncommon grace actively working in your life, you can forgive by trusting in God and find the strength to let go of the pain. You choose to forgive. God has placed in us a free will. That means that there is salvation from those deep places of hurt as we place those hurts in our heavenly Father's hands and surrender those hurts to Him. Be intentional to love as God has loved us. Be intentional to forgive as God has forgiven us.

Forgiveness is a process. Anytime along the way, you can choose to stop the process and carry the hurt on your own. However, our Savior with outstretched arms says, "Come and give your hurts to Me, lay your burdens, your hurts, your offenses at My feet and let Me take care of you." It is when we fall into the loving arms of our heavenly Father that we are set free from these hurts. He alone can give us the grace that it takes to truly forgive, releasing the hurt, the anger, the offense, the disappointment, and let it go.

Billy Graham said, *"In God's presence we are forgiven. In His arms I know who I am. I not only know who I am, I also know where I am going."*[17] I don't have to carry the weight of what I've done or what has been done to me. I am a treasure in the arms of Christ. God holds us accountable to Himself, and others are accountable to God in the end for whatever decisions they have made; even if those decisions have hurt us, angered us, or made us frustrated. We are not responsible for their decision, and we cannot make others bend to our wills. We are responsible to having our own will bent toward God. *In Him we have redemption (That is, our deliverance and salvation) through His blood, (Which paid the penalty for our sin and resulted in) the forgiveness and complete pardon of our sin, in accordance with the riches of His grace (Eph. 1:7, AMP).*

How many times do we need to forgive? Peter asked Jesus the same thing. "Then Peter came to Jesus and asked, 'Lord how many times shall I forgive my brother or sister who sins against me? Up to seven times?' Jesus answered, 'I tell you, not seven times, but seventy-seven times'" (Matt. 18:21–22, NIV). He is the God of not only second chances, but of third, fourth, and fifth chances. He never gives up on us, and He is always extending His love and uncommon grace to a sin-filled world. Forgive as many times as is needed. You feel justified to not forgive, but God commands us to forgive. Be challenged to lay down every unforgiven piece and lay it on the altar to be burned up. Controlling your anger and learning to forgive generously and quickly are parts of maintaining peace in your heart. Jesus extended forgiving grace through His life and death.

We continually make choices in our lives about how we will respond to circumstances. God pleads with us in His Word to make the right choices, but He still leaves the choice to us. In the book of Matthew, Jesus teaches us about forgiving grace.

Then his master summoned him and said to him, "You wicked servant! I forgave all that (great) debt because you pleaded with me. And should you not have had mercy on your fellow servant, as I had mercy on you?" And in anger his master delivered him to the jailers, until he should pay all his debt. So also, my heavenly Father will do to every one of you, if you do not forgive your brother from your heart. (Matt. 18:32–35, ESV)

Paul said, "I am not saying this because I am in need for I have learned to be content whatever the circumstances" (see Phil. 4:11, NIV). Paul had been beaten, put in prison, and shipwrecked, all for the sake of the gospel. Yet he lived a life of forgiveness, extending God's love to those who would kill him. Unforgiveness hurts you more than it hurts anyone else. God hears you even when you can't find the words to say. Do the right thing even when no one is looking. It is called integrity. God provides mercy and an uncommon grace to everyone; even those who have hurt or offended you. You are called to be like Jesus and forgive as He forgives (see Dan. 9:9, ESV).

Dig a Little Deeper

1. How do you find forgiveness for the things you have said or done?

    _____

    _____

    _____

2. How do you forgive others when you don't think they deserve forgiveness? How does unforgiveness affect your life and your testimony?

    _____

    _____

    _____

3. What did Jesus have to say about forgiveness?

_____

_____

_____

Daily Prayer

Lord may our daily prayer be that we will have a heart that forgives others as Christ has forgiven us. May truth and grace reside in our hearts of forgiveness. We pray that God will fill us with forgiving grace. Lord, let us step into Your presence, step into Your glory. Stir the water and bring healing to our hearts. Send hope for our hearts. Lord, You are leading us on this journey of faith. You wrap us in Your wraparound love. You are Lord of the harvest, and You bring our outcome. We trust in you. Amen.

"For all things are for your sakes, that the abundant grace might through the thanksgiving of many redound to the glory of God" (2 Cor. 4:15, KJV).

"We then, as workers together with him, beseech you also that ye receive not the grace of God in vain" (2 Cor. 6:1, KJV).

DAY 11

Glorious Grace

A S MY HUSBAND and I have traveled, we often stop at churches to pray and possibly attend a service. We have been blessed to spend time in the secret place within some of the most beautiful churches in the world. In a church in Vienna, Austria, we entered and went immediately to an area where we could kneel and pray. There was no one in the room. There was such a beautiful, peaceful, holy atmosphere in that magnificent church. We had been praying for a while in this place, thinking we were alone. We could feel an overwhelming, holy presence in that place, like a wind blowing on us and around us. We recognized the presence of God and Him alone. We had experienced a holy encounter in this place of God's glorious grace. As we turned to leave, we saw two nuns standing in the back of the church praying. I believe God brought them there to pray specifically for us, and I believe God heard and answered their prayers. If you are willing to open your heart, God will meet you there.

Can you remember a time when you first loved the Lord and knew His profound love for you? If we are to know God's glorious grace, we must press into His presence. Go back to your first encounter with the love of Jesus. Be abandoned to Him and focus on the one who first loved you. In Christ's letter to the church in Ephesus, He said, "But I have this against you: you have abandoned the passionate love you had for Me at the beginning" (Rev. 2:4, TPT). Jesus is referring to exclusive love that has first place in our heart above all else. In Psalm 91, the Psalmist tells us that God is the hope that holds us and that He will rescue us. His massive arms are wrapped around us to protect us. When we live our lives within the shadow of the Most High, our secret hiding place, we will always be shielded from harm through His glorious grace (see Psalm 91, TPT). He is calling us back to Him, our first love.

The word glorious is defined as being worthy or deserving of admiration, praise, and honor; having a striking beauty of splendor; delightful, wonderful, entitled to be great and worthy of high praise; magnificent, impressive, successful, and likely to be remembered. Grace is the free and unmerited favor of God, as manifested in the salvation of sinners and the bestowal of blessing. Mercy is compassion or forgiveness from someone who has the power to punish or forgive.

There is a place in our souls that words alone cannot touch; a place where the deeper issues of life are understood, where our spirits meet God's in an incredibly emotional and profoundly real way. An authentic love of God presses into Him. Be led and positioned by God through His presence and glorious grace. God is never in a hurry but always on time. When you withdraw to the secret place and are still before our heavenly Father, then He will put peace within you in every situation. Can you think of a time when you were overwhelmed by the presence of God and rested in His glorious grace?

You must seek His face, His presence, then power comes. If you leave out the presence, you are seeking power and signs. But if you are resting, dwelling in His presence, abiding under the shadow, then miracles and signs come (see Ps. 27:4–5, ESV). You must know God's ways. He reveals Himself through His manifested presence, His shekinah glory (see Exod. 33:19–23, ESV). Anything you do must be done because of being in His presence, or it will be done out of pride (see Isa. 40:31, ESV). Through His glorious grace, we see Him in all His glory.

There is a contingency to dwelling in the secret place. The Psalmist tells us to "Surrender your anxiety! Be silent and stop your striving and you will see that I am God. I am the God above the nations, and I will be exalted throughout the whole earth. Here He stands! The Commander! The mighty Lord of Angel Armies is on our side! The God of Jacob fights for us!" (Ps. 46:10–11, TPT). It is your responsibility to be in the secret place; it is God's responsibility to meet you there. In Hebrew *shasta* means to be quiet, at peace, rest undisturbed. "In returning and rest you shall be saved; in quietness and in trust shall be your strength" (see Isa. 30:15, ESV).

In the book of Ezekiel, the Lord declares: "I will show the holiness of my great name, which has been profaned among the nations, the name you have profaned among them. Then the nations will know that I am the Lord, declares the sovereign Lord, when I show myself holy through you before their eyes" (Ezek. 36:23, NIV). In the Psalm, God says: "Be still, and know that I am God, I will be exalted among the nations, I will be exalted in the earth" (Ps. 46:10, NIV). You have authority to take the gospel to the nations and to set men free. You may be a common man or woman, but you have been called to be uncommon. Every place the sole of your feet touches is under the authority of Jesus Christ. Through God the Father, Jesus, and the Holy Spirit, you are under authority, and you are given authority to change the world for God.

Do the works that please God. You must not be afraid to live by faith. You must proclaim the gospel personally, corporately, and globally through your lifestyle and your words. You as a Christian should be known by your love. You are to be recklessly abandoned to the gospel of Jesus Christ to go and tell the nations of His redeeming love and the glorious grace He has waiting for them. You are to be about the Heavenly Father's business. "Those who win souls are wise" (Prov. 11:30, NKJV).

Occupy the land with a heart for God and a love for people. Set their hope in God and do not forget the works of God. Keep before you the revelation of who God is and His character and characteristics. Don't let the enemy take your voice, your authority. Turn your ear to God for revelation and truth. God will bring revival to bring conviction and revelation. May His glorious grace overtake you. The power of the Holy Spirit gives you authority! Don't forget that the same power that raised Jesus is inside you! God shows Himself mighty in your midst. "For I know the plans I have for you, declares the Lord. Plans to prosper you and not to harm you, plans to give you hope and a future" (Jer. 29:11, NIV).

Dig a Little Deeper

1. How does God's glorious grace make you a world changer?

   _____

   _____

   _____

2. Have you experienced an encounter with God that has revealed His glorious grace?

   _____

   _____

   _____

3. Can you think of a time when God has led and positioned you through His presence and glorious grace?

   _____

   _____

   _____

   _____

Daily Prayer

Lord may our daily prayer be that we will be sensitive to Your Holy Spirit that souls may come to know the saving grace of Jesus Christ and that we will recognize it is time to harvest. Lord, fill us with your boldness to fulfill the assignments You have for our lives. May our lives be a life of prayer that we will know the seasons and times as we are still before You, Father God, listening to You, being guided by You. May all that we do be through You, for You, and with You! Thank you for the abundant life You have given us. Forgive us when we take Your blessings for granted. May we always trust in You. Amen.

"Which is come unto you, as it is in all the world; and bringeth forth fruit, as it doth also in you, since the day ye heard of it, and knew the grace of God in truth" (Col. 1:6, KJV).

"For the grace of God that bringeth salvation hath appeared to all men, teaching us that, denying ungodliness and worldly lusts, we should live soberly, righteously, and godly, in this present world" (Titus 2:11–12, KJV).

DAY 12

Abiding in Grace

O NE EVENING, WHILE in college, I was walking across the campus to the library. I was stopped by two young men who blocked my path and would not let me pass. One of them said, "I know you. You are that girl that claims to be a Christian. Are you that girl?" I answered, "Yes, I am a Christian. I believe in Jesus Christ." They began to laugh and pressed closer. I was remembering that a young woman had been raped the week before next to the science building, nor far from where we were standing. There was no one else around.

In that moment I had to decide if I was going to let fear overtake me or trust God. I felt a strong warmth rise inside of me, and I knew God was with me. The young men continued to taunt me and make jokes about me being a Christian. They said, "Do you really believe Jesus is real?" I responded that I knew Jesus was real because He lives in me. I know that He gave His life on a cross and died for my sins and that He arose from the dead and His Spirit continues to live in all that believe in Him. Now, I was very quiet and shy. It was completely out of my personality for me to speak so boldly. But in that moment, I knew that no matter what they did to me that I had to speak the truth.

One of the young men got close to me and spit on my face. I said to him, "I just want you to know that Jesus loves you and no matter what you do to me, I love you with the love of Jesus." I must admit, as I heard the words come out of my mouth, I couldn't believe what I was saying. I was shaking. But I was looking straight in their eyes. They shrugged their shoulders and said, "You are crazy." Then they walked away. I knew God had protected me. I prayed that God would burn the words in their hearts that I had said to them. I prayed that God would not let them sleep but would remind them of the encounter they had with me. I prayed for the Holy Spirit to pierce their hearts and bring them to know Him.

We walk through the time of trouble to the other side because He is with us. It is His presence that sees us through these times. It is during the time of trouble that His presence preserves, protects, and comforts us. Right at this very minute, during the hard realities and devasting circumstances, we must hold on to our Savior, knowing that our lives depend on God's abiding grace. It is with grace we more than survive; we thrive. As the Psalmist said, "Though I walk in the midst of trouble, You preserve my life, You stretch out your hand against the rath of my enemies, and Your right hand delivers me" (Ps. 138:7, ESV). "Even though I walk through the valley of the shadow of death, I will fear no evil, for You are with me, Your rod, and Your staff, they comfort me" (Ps. 23:4, ESV).

Our choices determine if God's hand will be outstretched to correct or to protect. The Psalmist declares, "Now I know that the Lord saves His anointed; He answers him from His holy heaven with the saving power of His right hand" (Ps. 20:6, ESV). When we find ourselves in times when we are unsure of what to say or what to do, we can always be sure that God is with us, and He pierces the hearts of humanity as we stand strong in our God and call out to Him as our Savior in those moments. "Then they cried to the Lord in their trouble, and He delivered them from their distress" (Ps. 107:6, ESV). "Save us and help us with Your right hand, that those You love may be delivered" (see Ps. 108:6, NIV).

Grace takes us beyond the common and brings the uncommon, the supernatural love of God, into our lives daily. Jesus was an uncommon man who brought uncommon grace to us through His life, His sacrifice on the cross, and His resurrection power. It is through this grace we find redemptive power to live an uncommon life. His presence takes away fear and gives us peace. Can you remember a time in your life that God's grace brought you peace in the middle of a difficult time? Do you automatically turn to God when you find yourself in tough times? Do you abide in His grace?

We are to be witnesses of Jesus Christ and share this gospel with the empowering of the Holy Spirit. Where your natural stops, the supernatural starts to equip and empower. Life is interrupted for a passionate purpose to share the gospel. *"Impossible is where God starts, and miracles are what He does."*[19] God asks us to do what seems impossible in the moment. The same spirit that raised Jesus from the dead lives inside of us making nothing impossible. There is limitless power in you to share the gospel and to bring life to others.

We are to be always stretching forward. Apprehend that which God has apprehended for you. His abiding grace provides power to do what you are unable to do on your own. Be fearless with a reverent fear of God, free from the expectation of men. We are to be radically abandoned to Christ. In Philippians, the scripture says, "And I am sure of this, that He who began a good work in you will bring it to completion at the day of Jesus Christ" (Phil. 1:6, ESV).

The story of Gideon gives us insight into how God uses whoever is willing to give their "yes". Gideon was hiding and secretly harvesting. God started with Gideon in his weakness, giving him a dream. He dreamed of a pitcher with lights rolling down a hill that knocked down the tents and all the Midianites fled. Gideon and his men placed lights in jars of clay and blew rams horns. He had a strategic plan of action. Gideon was the least in the house of Manasseh, but God used him mightily. God told him to go forth and conquer. God puts you in a hiding place, a cave, a tent, the side of a rock, to prepare you for his calling. He calls you to come out of the cave. "An angel appeared to Gideon and said: 'The Lord is with you mighty man of valor'" (Judg. 6:12, ESV). He called him what he wasn't yet. God is waiting on you to step up into your calling. His grace gives you the power to do what you are unable to do on your own. The excellency is in the power of God that rests in you.

On the cross, Jesus became sin that we might know the righteousness of God. Jesus died in our place. The world needs to know our Savior and the life He has provided for them. Be free from the expectation of what men say or think and know there is power in your words. Walk through the door of God's promises every day. Share the gospel with boldness. God says "when," not "if." Move forward aggressively with vision and purpose and a calling to share Jesus with this world. Life is going to throw all kinds of things your way, both good and bad, but know that our God is a loving God. He will always be in your corner. He is there to celebrate with you when things are going well, and to comfort you when you are struggling. During these times remember His promises.

Dig a Little Deeper

1. How does God's abiding grace help you to survive and thrive?

_____

_____

_____

2. How does God's abiding grace take us beyond the common to the uncommon?

_____

_____

_____

3. Can you recall a difficult time in your life when God's abiding grace brought you peace in the middle of a difficult time?

_____

_____

_____

Daily Prayer

May our daily prayer be that we will find a hiding place in Your shadow, Almighty God, that we might take refuge in You, under Your protection and guidance. Fill us, Lord, with Your grace and empower us to share the gospel. As the storm comes through, may our praise only come through stronger. Lord, may You provide protection and provision as we rest in Your abiding grace. May we be good stewards of all You place in our hands. We are so grateful for all You have given us. We are blessed indeed! Amen.

"John bore witness of Him, and cried, saying, this was He of whom I spoke, He that cometh after me is preferred before me: for He was before me. And of His fulness have all we received, and grace for grace. For the law was given by Moses, but grace and truth came by Jesus Christ" (John 1:15–17, KJV).

"And you, that were sometime alienated and enemies in your mind by wicked works, yet now hath He reconciled in the body of His flesh through death, to present you holy, and unblameable and unreproveable in his sight" (Col. 1:21–22, KJV).

DAY 13

Supernatural Grace

G OD'S SUPERNATURAL GRACE gives us strength and empowers us
to persevere in the most difficult times. During the storms we trust in
God to sustain us and see us through those times. It is after the storms that
we are challenged to continue to persevere. However, God also empowers
and strengthens us after the storms.

Several years ago, Baton Rouge, Louisiana, was flooded. Our family,
including my brother-in-law's home and church were flooded. My husband's
elderly parents were also caught in the middle of this flood. They escaped
the flood and got to higher ground with only a few of their precious belong-
ings. They were literally carried by their grandsons through the flooding
waters and were taken to higher ground. The family worked long hours
the following weeks and months to clean and salvage what they could of
their homes and the church. However, God provided His supernatural grace,
strength, and perseverance to restore their homes and the church. Many
people lost their homes and possessions due to the floods.

God is with you not only in the storm, but also in the aftermath. If we
are willing to persevere, God will provide His supernatural grace, giving us
hope to move forward, and He will restore what was lost. Jesus warned us
that difficult times would come. He also promised that He would never
leave us or forsake us. He fashions every event, even the most painful, into
our good. He gives us these promises to anchor our souls, even in the most
turbulent times.

Supernatural grace comes from supernatural power found from a deep
and abiding relationship with Christ Jesus. We should be in the great expectation mode. We should believe in impossibilities. Every day wake up to
expectation that Jesus has not given up on your situation. God is not taking

a picture of what you are doing. He is taking a picture of what you believe. We need to focus on what we can do and not on what we can't do. Jesus takes the language of fear, doubt, and unbelief and destroys it.

God waits until it is impossible for man. When you are pushed to your limit, when it is impossible for you; you know only God can do the impossible. In the book of Hebrews, we see that "Without faith it is impossible to please God" (Heb. 11:6, KJV). The attack from the enemy becomes stronger when you are about to be used by God, when your destiny is unfolding. Nothing is working until Jesus shows us the way. He provides help when it is hard to believe. God is provoking us to not give up. In the book of Hebrews, we see that "Now faith is the substance of things hoped for, the evidence of things not seen" (Heb. 11:1, KJV).

Jesus used what was common to show Himself to the people. Jesus called common men to follow Him (see Mark 1:16, ESV). Jesus's ministry was always to the people. Even what He poured into His inner circle was to build them for going out and taking the gospel to the people. This is kingdom vision. Supernatural Grace comes between purpose and power. God cannot agree with unbelief. God comes into agreement with faith and belief. It pleases Him when you pray in faith. Faith requires absolute obedience to God. We must be careful when we pray for something and do not get it, that we don't replace it with something else.

His voice is strong and is connected to His power. His voice, His words, break, shake, and flashes forth flames of fire. He promises to bless His people with peace. In His voice is also the sound of many waters (see Ps. 29, ESV). Let what was familiar become the unknown. Through His supernatural grace, we are prepared to love, lead, and bless. Be content in whatever state you are, whatever the call, whatever the challenge. Your weakness does not disqualify you from God's love. Call yourself what God calls you: loved, forgiven, strong, daughter, son, restored, healed.

His supernatural grace is sufficient. When He speaks; can you hear His voice in the thunder and roaring waves? Do you see His power in the lightning? Do you hear Him in the tiny whisper, saying, "I am with you"? Do you hear Him when He calls your name? Do you recognize His voice? He makes a way that we might exceed the limits of mediocre to be exceptional and extraordinary.

He makes a way through our fear. The Psalmist says, "When I am afraid, I put my trust in You" (Ps. 56:3, ESV). Do you believe God for the supernatural in your life? You can go through the storm with joy because you are victorious. I have heard it said, some things assigned to your past are not assigned to your future. Grace carries you in the process. The scriptures tell us in 2nd Corinthians, "My Grace is sufficient for you for my power is made perfect in weakness" (2 Cor. 12:9, NIV).

We are charged to advance the kingdom. We are to be world changers and history makers. Finish strong for God. Be radical for God and let your desire to follow Jesus become an obsession. Stay single-minded and be like Jesus. You don't have to be great to start, but you must start to be great. Serve with radical excellence. Supernatural grace fills the gap between promise and fulfillment. On the third day after Jesus was crucified, two men were walking on the road to Emmaus. Jesus was walking with them, but they did not recognize Him until He broke bread with them. We all need to have that Emmaus experience when Christ reveals Himself to us (see John 20:18, NIV).

A supernatural shift takes place in your heart and spirit when Christ reveals Himself to you. It changes your life, and you are no longer the same. Lost and broken becomes changed to the redeemed of the Lord. As we yield to the Lord, a shift from fear to faith occurs. Pray and believe for a change in your very core, trusting God in the middle of the challenge.

The disciples had fished all night and had not caught any fish. Jesus told them to cast their nets on the other side, and as they did, they caught so many fish, their nets broke. Jesus calls us as present-day disciples to cast our nets on the other side of the Sea of Galilee. He can do the impossible for us. We are disciples whom He disciples. God calls us to be champions and leaders, giving our best (see Luke 21:19, ESV).

Don't be a distant watcher. You may be too far away to hear His whisper. Everybody wants power and authority but not the cost. Draw close to God. Hear His voice and know His call for your life. His Spirit lives in us to empower us to be witnesses to the world. We have the same flesh and blood as the early church. We need to get the same vision as the early church. They found Jesus, and they instantly followed Him. We must have the same zeal, the same fire, in our bellies.

Dig a Little Deeper

1. Where does supernatural grace come from?

_____

_____

_____

2. What does it mean to advance the kingdom and be a world changer?

_____

_____

_____

3. How does supernatural grace help us in difficult times?

_____

_____

_____

Daily Prayer

Father God may our daily prayer be that You will place within us the supernatural grace to expect the unexpected and to rely on the supernatural to do what only You can do. We thank You for the gift of the Holy Spirit that always leads and guides us as we place our trust in You. Your supernatural grace brings us perfect peace in the middle of the storm. You remind us that we are overcomers and victorious in every battle. We long to be drawn closer to You each day, and as we lay our heads down to sleep at night, we thank You for Your supernatural grace that always makes a way for us. Amen.

"But none of these things move me. Neither count
I my life dear unto myself, so that I might finish
my course with joy, and the ministry, which I
have received of the Lord Jesus, to testify the
gospel of the grace of God" (Acts 20:24, KJV).

"For if ye forgive men their trespasses, your heavenly
Father will also forgive you" (Matt. 6:14, KJV).

DAY 14

Grace Under Fire

WHEN SOUTH KOREA was liberated, and they once again had religious freedom, a liberated Holy Ghost fire spread across the country. Prayer was the key. When we were last in South Korea, we saw the power of prayer as the home group pastors prayed over the people in their home groups. As they prayed, it was like fire resting over their heads. They were being prepared for the coming week. They live with the constant threat of war and a constant hope for peace. We also saw them in the marketplace, singing, dancing and telling the people of the saving grace of Jesus Christ. The buses in Seoul, Korea, only run one way on Sunday mornings. The buses are all filled with people going to church. It is the fire of God that has consumed their hearts.

When in Israel, we were in the Upper Room. As we prayed, we were reminded of the fire of God that consumes and we experienced the power of Pentecost. Through the fire of God released at the first Pentecost those in the upper room were ignited to be faithful, courageous, and uncompromising. They were filled with wisdom and anointing. "Suddenly a wind came into the room and tongues as of fire appeared over their heads and rested on them" (see Acts 2, ESV). If God's fire can consume your tongue, your speech, He can consume your life.

Stir the passion for His presence, passion for His holiness, and passion to pursue Him. God sent His best, Jesus, to bring out the best in us. He places the fire of the Holy Spirit in us to cleanse us, to provide the power for the manifestation of miracles, and to have boldness to be witnesses. We can also see the fire within flowing through the prophetic. The Holy Spirit resides in us, so the fire is now within us, anointing us to be used for demonstration of His power. The anointing is represented by the oil. God's holy presence, the Holy Spirit, is represented by the fire. When the oil and the fire are combined, the fire intensifies. To keep the fire going, it must be blown on and stirred. May we invite the Holy Spirit to breathe life into us and stir up His anointing in us.

The mouth speaks of what is in the heart. What you say is what you believe, and what you believe is what you become. It is the filling of the fire of the Holy Spirit that completes us and moves us into our destiny. In Acts we see that "You will receive power when the Holy Spirit has come upon you and you will be my witnesses in Jerusalem, and all Judea, and Samaria and to the end of the earth" (Acts 1:8, ESV). We were created to live extraordinary lives. We are to be bold, full of faith, and power.

Jesus is the ultimate gift you can receive. When we are saved, God, His Spirit comes to live in us. The baptism of the Holy Spirit is a baptism of fire that consumes your mind, will, and emotions. We always have a choice, but the fire gives us clear, holy choices. Fire is for unlocking our mouths to speak in a spiritual language and for power to be witnesses.

We, who are the redeemed of the Lord, are not of this world but of His kingdom, and our identity and citizenship is in Him. This is what gives us the authority to have dominion in this world. We see in Hebrews, "For God is a consuming fire" (Heb. 12:29, ESV). The fiery nature of God is the essence of who we are in Christ Jesus (see Matt.5:3–10, ESV). We are not to be mediocre. Rekindle the hunger for the holy in your life and seek out God's destiny for you. The word intense means to be a fire, an intense fire, to give great attention to the matter, and be focused and attentive. Intensity gives value to the purpose.

We are sanctified by going through the fire. We are to live on purpose to do the right thing. Fire consumes everything in sight. All fire is hot and leaves a mark or scar if touched. The scriptures declare that our God is a consuming fire. God reveals Himself through fire. We are to shift into an intense drive toward excellence in every part of our lives and ministry. Excellence is considered beyond, surpassing, the ordinary. It is a continuously moving target that can be pursued through actions of integrity and is a forerunner to purpose being fulfilled.

The fire brings transformation even to the most hopeless and seemingly impossible circumstances. People who keep the fire of God burning on the altar of their hearts carry this fire with them wherever they go. We carry inside us an all-consuming fire. We are fire carriers. We are not to let the fire of God go dim. We see in Isaiah that God's glory shines as a light:

"Shine, for your light has come, and the glory of the Lord has risen upon you. For behold, darkness shall cover the earth, and thick darkness the peoples; but the Lord will arise upon you, and His glory will be seen upon you. And nations shall come to your light, and kings to the brightness of your rising" (Isa. 60:1–3, ESV).

We are to be burning brightly with the fire of God inside us. We are simply containers carrying the fire and oil of the anointing to the world. We are to seek after the fire of God in our lives. As we see in Jeremiah, "You will seek Me and find Me when you seek Me with all your heart" (Jer. 29:13, ESV). May we be carriers of the fire and start fires wherever we go, changing the landscape in the lives and hearts of people. When we hunger and thirst after God, desperately seeking Him, we find Him, and He pours out His Spirit (fire) in us to take to a desperate world. He is the God of more than enough. As we lay ourselves on God's altar, He burns away all that is not of Him and consumes us with Himself, His character, His nature, His holiness. Jesus came to bring radical changes to the world. He came to bring love, compassion, and truth. We are to be radical change agents in this world with the fire of God burning brightly in us.

On September 11, 2001, my husband, Joe, was working in Niagara Falls, New York. After the attack on the twin towers, all transportation came to a halt. My husband walked to a church near his hotel. Several others came into the church, and they began to pray together. They were strangers God had drawn together to pray and strengthen one another at one of our nation's most difficult time. At ground zero a church opened its doors and provided physical and spiritual help for those coming out of the ruins. First responders and others began to come into the church from the rubble covered in smoke and dirt, some injured and bleeding. Volunteers in the church washed them, fed them, gave them a place to rest and prayed for them.

We need to recognize that God himself through His Son, Jesus, has come to take residence in us. We carry Jesus to a lost and hopeless world. We bring hope to the hopeless and light to a dark world. There is no sin too great, no need too big for God. Jesus Christ died and rose again to bring salvation to this world. We must always stay focused on this truth to bring radical change to the world.

Dig a Little Deeper

1. What is meant by "We are sanctified by the fire"?

\
\
\

2. What is meant by "We are fire carriers"?

\
\
\

3.   What kind of transformation does the fire bring?

_____

_____

_____

Daily Prayer

Lord, may You give us words (fire words) to arouse a sleeping world. May we be a voice crying out the gospel to the lost. May we carry the fire of Your Holy Spirit in us so that we will testify to the world of the Redeemer. God, grant us a mind free of worry, a heart free of sadness, and a body free of sickness. Lord, place a fire deep inside us that we will want more of You and be consumed with taking Your Gospel to the world. May we carry good news of life and freedom. Lord, give us strength to continue our journeys. Our lives are in Your hands. Amen.

"Therefore, if any man be in Christ, he is a new creature: old things are passed away; behold, all things are become new" (2 Cor. 5:17, KJV).

"For all have sinned, and come short of the glory of God; Being justified freely by His grace through the redemption that is in Christ Jesus" (Rom. 3:23–24, KJV).

DAY 15

Refreshing Grace

G OD IS A river of refreshing strength and endurance. God promises to be with us and to help us. Out of the depths of God's Spirit flows rivers of living water. The Psalmist tells us, "There is a river whose streams make glad the city of God, the holy habitation of the Most High" (Ps. 46:4, ESV). There must be refreshing times in our lives to bring restoration of our physical, mental, and emotional health. God is our strength and refuge.

There is a river of anointing. To be full of Him, we must be empty of ourselves. As we release every part of ourselves to the Lord, then He comes and breathes His life into us. The river of anointing refreshes, restores, rebuilds, replenishes, refortifies, and requalifies us. Like fresh water for a thirsty and parched soul, His Spirit quenches and satisfies. The anointing places a strength that is supernatural, making the ordinary extraordinary.

I have heard it said, one day we will hear the behind-the-scenes stories of what went on in our behalf during the hardest moments of our lives. Then we will realize the unfathomable, strong ways heaven surrounded us every step! So be encouraged; the drama you see pales in comparison to what you can't see! Heaven fights for you and yours! You are not alone!

My husband and I have been a part of Dwelling Place Church International for the past ten years. I have also been a part of The International Institute of Mentoring. We have seen our pastors serve as evangelists, prophets, pastors, teachers, mentors, counselors, authors, conference speakers, singers, songwriters, and so much more. We have been in awe of their strength and personal compassion for others and their incredible work ethic. They also place a high priority on family, their daughters, and their marriage. My husband and I have had numerous conversations questioning how they are able to do what they do. Recently I was reading the book *Stand Strong,* by Judy Jacobs, and I gained a little insight into their secret.

There is a story in the book *Stand Strong* by Judy Jacobs where she says: "She had just returned home after preaching and singing and ministering for two weeks, covering several time zones and multiple services. She was exhausted. Pastor Jamie Tuttle asked her to take a shower and go to bed. He would take care of the girls. As she was preparing to go to sleep, the Holy Spirit spoke to her. He asked her to come away with Him. Physically she was exhausted, and her body was saying go to sleep. But she obeyed the Holy Spirit. She said that as she worshiped, the sweetest presence of God infiltrated her body and spirit."[20] I believe she received a refreshing right from the throne of God. She had been faithful in ministry and God was faithful to restore her.

When we no longer stand in our own abilities; but depend on God alone, He refreshes and restores. All that we are is because of whose we belong. The Psalmist best explains this refreshing grace when he says, "God is our refuge and strength, an ever-present help in trouble. Therefore, we will not fear, though the earth gives way, and the mountain falls into the heart of the sea, though its waters roar and foam and the mountains quake with their surging" (Ps. 46:1–3, NIV). He is our strength when our own strength fails us. He is our safe place where we can abide in Him.

Whether you serve or lead, you will find yourself in times of loneliness and isolation. Moses is an example of a servant leader who tried to do it all himself. There are seasons that require us to wait, rest, and be refreshed. Moses said, "I cannot carry all these people by myself; the burden is too heavy for me" (Num. 11:14, NIV). God sends people into our lives to help and partner with us. We also need to give ourselves permission to take time for refreshing.

The disciples were on the Sea of Galilee in a fishing boat. Jesus went up on the mountainside to pray. Perhaps Jesus was having a time of refreshing. Jesus walked on the water toward the boat. The disciples did not know what to expect. Those who knew Jesus the longest were afraid. Jesus was reaching out to them to walk out on the water and to come to him. Jesus was challenging them to step toward that which they did not know. Of the twelve, only one was willing to step out onto the water. That one was Peter who stepped out of the boat and began walking on the water toward Jesus. Peter turned away from everything familiar and put his trust in Jesus. In that moment, he began to experience the supernatural (see Mark 6, NIV). In that moment, Peter went from a common man to an uncommon man. This experience was all about Peter trusting Jesus. When we trust Jesus as Peter did, we are refreshed, strengthened, and empowered.

The disciples were not eager to take a risk. If you take your eyes off your Life Giver, everything begins to crumble. When Peter took his eyes off Jesus, he began to sink. The Almighty, all powerful, able to walk out onto the water God is there, reaching out to him. In the sinking, Jesus reaches down and pulls Peter up. Do not take your eyes off Jesus during the challenge. When you feel weak, exhausted, overextended and your faith is challenged this is when you reach out to Jesus. He is the only one who truly refreshes and strengthens you.

Refreshing comes when we press into Jesus. You are chosen of God. Your name is engraved in His hand. His assignment is engraved on your heart. Spend time in the deep compassions and tender mercies of the Lord. It is there you will find your refreshing. There are times of refreshing found in the presence of the Lord that renews your heart and mind. As Luke wrote in the book of Acts: "Repent therefore and be converted, that your sins may be blotted out, so that times of refreshing may come from the presence of the Lord, and He may send Jesus Christ, who was preached to you before, whom heaven must receive until the times of restoration of all things, which God has spoken by the mouth of all His holy prophets since the world began" (Acts 3:19–21, NKJV).

Dig a Little Deeper

1. How do we bring refreshing grace into our lives?

_____

_____

_____

2. What is the purpose of refreshing times?

_____

_____

_____

3. Can you think of a time of refreshing in your life?

_____

_____

_____

Daily Prayer

Lord, let our daily prayer be that we will walk in this river of life, that we will pursue You in all we do. May we rely on all that You are and not on ourselves to accomplish Your purpose for our lives. May we find life in You who gave Your life and Your refreshing grace. Lord, I pray for those in need of repentance and conversion, that their sins may be erased so that times of refreshing may come to them from Your presence. We are so thankful for Your guidance each day and bringing times of refreshing in our lives. Amen.

"Let your speech be always with grace, seasoned
with salt, that ye may know how ye ought
to answer every man" (Col. 4:6, KJV).

"He hath not dealt with us after our sins; nor
rewarded us according to our iniquities. For as
heaven is high above the earth, so great is His mercy
toward them that fear Him" (Ps. 103:10–11, KJV).

DAY 16

The Process of Grace

MY HUSBAND, JOE, and I taught a Sunday School class of eighth and ninth graders for two years. The six teenage students initially did not want to attend the class; this was very clear by their attitudes. But we knew God had led us to teach this class. We prayed over these students each week for over two years. We could not see any change in them at that time. However, we were confident that God was doing a work in their hearts. Seven years later, five of the six students had become full-time missionaries. One of them came back to thank us for speaking into his life.

You may not see the evidence of your obedience immediately, but God is faithful to His Word. Through His sovereign grace He took these young men and women and has positioned them in ministry and is using them greatly. It was the process of grace that prepared each one of these individuals for their purpose to be fulfilled.

We are God's treasured possession, His precious jewels. To be a treasured possession is to be personal property or to belong to someone. As we yield our hearts to the Lord, we become His possession. We belong to Him. We go through a process of grace that brings us to a place that we can be used of God. Just as He bestowed on King David His splendor and majesty, He bestows His splendor and majesty on those who partake in His life. As the scriptures say, "Through the victories you gave, His glory is great; You have bestowed on him splendor and majesty" (Ps. 21:5, NIV).

Through God's grace we are His treasured possessions, precious jewels, shining with splendor. The Psalmist describes it like this: "Praise the Lord, O my soul. O Lord my God, You are very great; You are clothed with splendor and majesty" (Ps. 104:1, NIV). We must yield to the process of being purified and refined. We are to be precious jewels, cut, refined, polished, and set apart so that the light reflects in such a way as to draw others to know that light that dwells inside of us. God is making you into a precious jewel to be used greatly shining for Him. What if the precious stone said to the jeweler, "Stop! You cannot cut on me," then those beautiful facets that makes that jewel to shine would not be there. Those who love Jesus are precious jewels that time cannot dim. Every jewel must go through the process. It is all about God's process of grace that prepares us. We must dig deep in God's Word to be a precious jewel that shines brightly for Him.

Down in the crust of the earth, toward the region of fire and molten rock, the worker in a mine faced darkness, depth, danger, depression, and sometimes death, to bring to the light silver from its veins, chunks of gold and gemstones. The tiniest, most fragile jewels are those most deeply buried. Mining means digging into the earth for treasure that has been hidden from man since the world began. It is a world without sunlight, a world of tunnels and passageways, crevices, pits and hiding places. In the coal mines are hidden jewels that must stay hidden away waiting for the right time to be brought out into the light.

The keeper of the jewels has great responsibility to take care, make provisions, and keep safe the jewels. The search for the jewels is timely and costly. They are polished to give perfect touches. The stone is then taken above ground. In a gem cutter's workshop, the stone is gripped in a vise, cut with a saw, ground with a coarse wheel, sanded, polished with tin oxide, and pierced with a drill.[21]

Nothing is ever made easy. We are polished by love, integrity, hard work, and discipline; reinforced by scripture, prayer, and worship. In Malachi we see God as the jeweler: "He shall sit as a refiner and purifier of silver" (Mal. 3:3, NIV). God works with souls like a jeweler works with gems. Once he finds and brings them to the light, they are cut, polished, and placed in a setting of His choice.

Christ is the light that lights the world. We are of great value, more precious than rubies. The size, the cut, the clarity, the rarity of the stone determines its value. Jesus, the stone the builders rejected, overcame rejection. The scripture tells us, "That no one be moved by these afflictions. For you yourselves know that we are destined for this" (1 Thess. 3:3, ESV). We see in the scriptures that we are His precious jewels. "Precious jewels which they stripped off" (see 2 Chron. 20:25, KJV). Whether a choice jewel, a starry cluster, or a precious gem, it is in the hands of the jeweler that the brilliance is brought out in each one. It is through the burning, the refining, the purifying, that God's glory is seen in the gold, and it is through the cutting away of the stone, making each facet by the jeweler's hands that we see His glory shine in such majesty and brilliance.

I asked our seven-year-old grandson, Levi, if he could travel to anywhere in the world, where would he go? He quickly said, "Israel." I asked him why he had chosen Israel. He replied, "I want to go to the tomb. You know, where they put Jesus after He died on the cross." I said, "Oh so you want to go to the places where Jesus went when He was on the earth." He replied, "Yes. But mostly I want to go to the tomb. I want to walk in it and see if Jesus's body is still there." I thought about his answer during the next few days. I put in perspective that this is a seven-year-old's understanding of the crucifixion and resurrection. I also realized this was a matter of faith.

God reminded me that as we grow in His grace, we also grow in faith. Levi is no different than most of us. We want to see it, touch it, and feel it to believe it is real. But faith requires us to have relationship with God that is all about trusting and believing without seeing it, touching, or feeling. This process of grace is essential for our growth and solidifying our relationship with our Savior. As we go through this process of grace, we come into full understanding that Jesus died on a cross for our sins and that He has extended to us grace that we might be redeemed. The resurrection is also His grace extended to us because His everlasting, resurrected life made a way for us to have eternal life. Levi's desire to see an empty tomb is the very basis of our faith and belief in a risen Savior.

Dig a Little Deeper

1. What is the process we must go through to shine as precious jewels for God?

    _____

    _____

    _____

2. Why is it important to go through the process of grace to fully understand the power of Christ's death and resurrection in us?

    _____

    _____

    _____

3. What could happen if you do not go through this process of grace and rely on your talents and abilities?

    _____

    _____

    _____

Daily Prayer

Lord may our daily prayer be: "Every morning I lay out the pieces of my life on the altar and wait for your fire to fall upon my heart" (Ps. 5:3, TPT). Forgive us, Lord, for the times we trust in our own abilities instead of trusting You. Forgive us, Lord, for the times we have been impatient instead of waiting on Your timing. We are so thankful for the ways You have revealed Your Word and will to us. Hold us close as we follow You. May all we do be for Your glory and honor. At the end of our lives may You say, "Well done." Amen.

"Now our Lord Jesus Christ himself, and God,
even our Father, which hath loved us, and hath
given us everlasting consolation and good
hope through grace" (2 Thess. 2:16, KJV).

"As every man hath received the gift, even so
minister the same one to another, as good stewards
of the manifold grace of God" (1 Pet. 4:10, KJV).

DAY 17

Anointed Grace

T HE SCRIPTURES SHOW us that Jesus is the Anointed One, the Messiah. "The Spirit of the Lord is upon me, because He has anointed me to preach the gospel to the poor; He has sent me to heal the broken-hearted, to proclaim liberty to the captives and recovery of sight to the blind, to set at liberty those who are oppressed; to proclaim the acceptable year of the Lord" (Luke 4:18–21, NKJV Spirit-Filled Life Bible). Jesus boldly claims to be the promised Messiah, and His defined ministry here becomes the ongoing essence of the good news of the gospel of the kingdom of God.

Pastor Jamie Tuttle says this about the anointing: *"The anointing is simply the fuel of God's presence on one for the purpose of the establishment of God's kingdom. It is what some call unction, and it precedes supernatural manifestation and demonstration of God through His people."*[22]

God's anointing comes with worship. Worship is an experience and relationship with the Lord. Worship is an intimate time with God. The deepest part of you has relationship with the deepest part of God. Through that relationship, we find anointing for the uncommon life He has called us to live. We are anointed to follow through with God's assignments, have godly character, and be used in warfare. We must go before Him with a pure heart. *"The anointing purifies you for your purpose."*[23]

"Enter into His gates with thanksgiving, and into His courts with praise be thankful unto Him and bless His name" (Ps. 100:4, KJV). We are empowered through praise in the outer court and worship in the inner court. But it is in the Holy of Holies where we find His anointing and His presence. Jesus tells us: "But the hour cometh, and now is when the true worshippers shall worship the Father in spirit and in truth: For the Father seeks such to worship Him" (John 4:23, KJV). We find God's anointing through worship. We are realigned with God's purpose and plan for us through worship. Worship enables our hearts to be tender toward God and to allow Him to change us from the inside out. Worship changes the attitude and atmosphere of the heart. His presence creates the heart of worship.

God inhabits the praise of His people. The Psalmist says, "Yet I know that you are most holy; it's indisputable. You are God-enthroned surrounded with songs, living among the shouts of praise of Your princely people" (Ps. 22:3, TPT). God dwells where there is worship and praise. It is in worship that the sound of heaven is revealed and communion with God is found. That sound changes our hearts, minds, and will.

> *"Anointing is joy, passion, power, glory, confidence, boldness, and authority. It makes you cry. It makes you laugh. It gives you righteous indignation. It is the power to preach, sing, witness, testify, and do spiritual warfare. It is peace. It comes suddenly, and it takes time. It is meek and it is strong."[24]*

In the book of Acts, we see God bring freedom for Paul and Silas through worship. "And at midnight Paul and Silas prayed and sang praises unto God; and the prisoners heard them. And suddenly there was a great earthquake, so that the foundation of the prison was shaken and immediately the doors were opened, and everyone's bands were loose" (Acts 16:25–26, KJV). God is our authority. He gives us dominion and authority over the enemy and has made a way for us to have victory through the shedding of His blood. God has given us our worship as a weapon. As we surrender to God, fear is overcome by freedom.

We are a part of a revolutionary purpose and plan of Almighty God through His anointing. He gives us the authority to prevail over every plan of the enemy. God's plan is that we have dominion over every aspect of our lives. The Word of the Lord will always prevail. Don't just fight—fight to win! Then, my friends, because of God's great mercy to us, offer yourselves as a living sacrifice to God, dedicated to His service and pleasing to Him. The anointing enables us to arise in our destiny, empowers us to be witnesses and invades our worship. This is the true anointed worship you should offer. I have heard it said, "True worship is to let your worship be to God and Him alone."

The anointing is to set apart a person for a particular work or service (see Isa. 61:1, KJV). All who are Christ's disciples are said to be anointed; they are God's very own, set apart and commissioned for service. Priests, kings, and prophets were anointed. Oil was poured on the head of the person being anointed (see Exod. 29:7, KJV). Kings were set apart through the ritual of anointing, which was performed by a prophet, who acted in God's power and authority (see 1 Sam. 15:1, KJV). In the New Testament, anointing was frequently used in connection with healing (see Mark 6:13, KJV).

> *The anointing also refers to the anointing of the Holy Spirit which brings understanding. The anointing is for everyone who believes in Jesus Christ. The anointing occurs physically with oil; To anoint, to rub with oil, especially to consecrate someone or something. But there is also a spiritual anointing, as the Holy Spirit anoints a person's heart and mind with the love and truth of God. When there is reference to a service that it was an anointed service, it is referring to the presence of God with power in the service.*[25]

I have witnessed the anointing as the presence of God has filled the room through corporate worship and prayer. The gifts of the Spirit are evidenced through the anointing. I have experienced God's anointing power in crusades where hundreds had gathered ready to receive from an anointed Evangelist. At times, the anointing can be so strong you can feel God's presence physically; it is like walking through smoke. I have also experienced the anointing in private prayer times. It is in these times that God speaks clearly to our hearts. God desires to touch the hearts of His people, and He desires for His people to long for Him. The anointing is that conduit God, the one and only true God, uses to meet with His people and meet their needs.

When Peter came to the temple to pray, the people would line up so that as he passed, they would be healed by his shadow (see Acts 5:15, NKJV). *"It was actually the Presence of God upon him, for the anointing is a person."*[26] We also see in the scriptures when a sick woman thought if she could just touch the hem of Jesus's garment, she would be made well. She touched the hem of Jesus' garment, and she was healed. It is thought that the woman touched the Tallit the tassels hanging from the prayer shawl. *"Generally speaking, the anointing is the power of God to accomplish His purposes, regardless of the sphere of your ministry."*[27]

Dig a Little Deeper

1. Define anointing.

_____

_____

_____

2. What is the purpose of the anointing?

_____

_____

_____

3. Describe a time you witnessed the anointing.

_____

_____

_____

Daily Prayer

Lord may our daily prayer be that we will seek Your presence in our lives. May we walk in Your anointing that we will be empowered to be witnesses and share the gospel of Jesus Christ with others. May we be anointed to follow through with Your assignments, have godly character, and be used in warfare. Lord, set us apart for service and anoint us to fulfill Your calling on our lives. May we be anointed to be purified for Your purpose. Lord, may we live a life of anointed prayer. Place Your mantle on us that we will bring the Gospel to the lost and brokenhearted. Amen.

"If we confess our sins, He is faithful and just
to forgive us our sins, and to cleanse us from
all unrighteousness" (1 John 1:9, KJV).

"There is only one strong, safe, and secure place for
me; it's in God alone and I love Him! He's the one who
gives me strength and skill for battle. He is my shelter
of love and my fortress of faith, who wraps Himself
around me as a secure shield. I hide myself in this one
who subdues enemies before me" (Ps. 144:1–2, TPT).

DAY 18
Authentic Grace

WHEN IN IRELAND, we saw sheep along the countryside. We noticed that there was a red mark on the upper back part of each one of the sheep. We talked with a shepherd who was taking care of the sheep. He told us that the red mark was a brand that showed who owned these sheep. You could see the brand went through the wool and into the skin of the sheep. So even the sheared sheep had the brand. There were a few sheep separated from the other sheep. These few sheep were being fattened up. The shepherd was making sure they had access to the best field and water. The shepherd was driving the sheep to an area closer to the barn area for the evening. The Psalmist tells us in Psalm 23 that the Good Shepherd, Jesus, takes care of His sheep. When we openly love people and open our hearts to Jesus, we then have His brand. We know that we belong to Jesus and follow Him. We are living an authentic Christian life when we stay close to the Shepherd.

Break forth on purpose and live an authentic life. We pray, "God give me courage to hear and follow." We are to walk in excellence, not in our own strength, but in the strength we find in following Jesus Christ. Live a life of holiness, wholeness, and boldness. That is what makes you authentic.

The shepherd will put oil on the head of the sheep to keep the bugs and flies away from the sheep's eyes. The oil also keeps the sheep from being trapped in the barbed wire fences. With the oil on his head, the sheep can more easily pull out of the fencing without causing him damage. The Good Shepherd, Jesus, puts the anointing oil on our heads to call us to a sanctified life, a holy authentic life with no hidden sins.

You are called to be significant influencers (see Rom. 12:1–2, NIV). Jesus came to set us free from being normal. Your uniqueness makes you a peculiar person. Dare to be different (see Acts 2:4, NIV). Jesus's mantel is for each one of us to bring hope and life to the world. His blood poured out marks us and gives us our brand. You've got to stand out and be bold. Know who you are and to whom you belong.

What has God gifted in you? Your gift creates a place for you. Be pliable and flexible. God will move beyond your ability. Your passion and testimony will make a way for you to overcome. What has God done in and through you? This is your testimony. God will equip you for what you can do. Your calling is your passion and testimony (see John 14:21, NIV). God gives you the power, authority, and boldness to walk out you're gifting and calling.

When in Malahide, Ireland, during the day, I took walks into the nearby countryside and villages. It rained every day during the time we were there. I was walking to a nearby village and saw this great mist hovering over the water. You could not see even a foot in front of you in the mist. As I was walking, the mist began to slowly lift. After some time, I could see there was land in the middle of the water. But I could not make out anything else. After a bit more time, I could see that this land was an island in the middle of the water.

I continued to walk, and the mist continued to lift. After a while I could see that there were golfers on the island. Finally, the mist was lifted, and I could see this well-known golf course with numerous players. It was a quiet beautiful golf course. What had been hidden was now completely revealed. I share this to say that we often take things at face value and miss what is there. Sometimes we just need to keep walking until all is revealed. What does this have to do with being authentic or living in authentic grace? We need to seek after God to reveal Himself and His ways to us so that we truly walk in His authenticity. He longs for an authentic relationship with us.

When Jesus saw Jerusalem, He had compassion (see Isa. 11:1, NIV). May we have compassionate hearts for the world. If you cut off a piece of the olive tree, a new shoot will grow up and produce fruit: olives. We are connected to Jesus like a vine that produces fruit (see Ps. 128:3, NIV). The olives are placed in the oil press. This is what happened to Jesus. He was pressed so that the oil, representing His anointing and presence, and His life could be poured forth. We all have a personal calling. We were called out of darkness into the light, and we are called to follow a risen Savior. Stay the course God has called you to, always be pressing forward. Let your walk be authentic. Be willing to be pressed so that all that is not of Jesus is pulled away in the press and the oil of His Spirit is poured out of you.

Focus forward. We must keep our vision and purpose always set before us. Jesus sets the example for us as He says, "I have set my face like a flint" (see Isa. 50:7, ESV). "Jesus said to him, 'No one who puts his hand to the plow and looks back is fit for the kingdom of God'" (Luke 9:62, ESV). We are to live authentically with hearts of love. We are to lose our old minds and be renewed by Christ Jesus. I love how Paul expresses what it is to follow Christ. "Brethren, I count not myself to have apprehended; but one thing I do, forgetting those things which are behind and reaching forward unto those things which are ahead" (Phil. 3:13, NKJ). When you base your worth and identity in your relationship to Christ, you are freed from the expectations of others, and that allows you to serve at your best.

The key to walking in authentic grace is to simply "Set your minds on things above, and not on earthly things" (Col. 3:2, NIV). Fix your thoughts on Jesus. "Therefore, prepare your minds for action; be self-controlled; set your hope fully on the grace to be given you when Jesus Christ is revealed" (1 Pet. 1:13, NIV). Our hearts' desires need to be one with our Heavenly Father's desires for us. To be one with God, we must yield our wants and desires to Him. Through His Word, our minds are renewed daily. God promises us a heart that is filled with His love and a mind that is at peace when we are yielded to Him. He breaks through the confusion, misinformation, and lies to bring truth and stability.

Surrender to freedom. To be an authentic overcomer, you must cast down thoughts. He is truth. We are to live truth and stand strong. Fear, anxiety, and stress are lies. Truth empowers us to live an authentic Christian life above the lies. Others are watching us to see if we live an authentic life for Jesus Christ. Do we live what we say? As ambassadors of the Gospel, we must keep our hearts and minds focused on Jesus and His assignment on our life. That assignment is first to take the Gospel to the lost to those who are hurting and in need of a Savior. We are called to go and tell but also to go and show a life consumed with living out the Gospel, by living an uncommon life with uncommon grace.

Dig a Little Deeper

1. Describe what it means to live an authentic Christian life.

_____

_____

_____

2. How are we to be significant influencers to others?

_____

_____

_____

3. What is the key to walking in authentic grace?

_____

_____

_____

Daily Prayer

Father may our daily prayer be that Your thoughts would be our thoughts, that we might see our circumstances through Your eyes. Let our minds focus on Your precepts that we might be renewed. We are so thankful that You have revealed your power and presence in our lives. Thank you for Your power to run this race of faith. With You, all things are possible. You have already made a way for us before the challenge comes. I give You all my thanks and praise. Give us wisdom to walk in Your ways. May we walk authentically in Your grace. Lord, all the glory is Yours and Yours alone. Amen.

"And Stephen, full of faith and power,
did great wonders and miracles among
the people" (Acts 6:8, KJV).

"And now brethren, I commend you to God, and to
the word of His grace, which is able to build you
up, and to give you an inheritance among all of
them which are sanctified" (Acts 20:32, KJV).

DAY 19

Ambassadors of Grace

RECENTLY WE HAD the opportunity to meet a pastor and his wife who had narrowly escaped Russia's invasion of Ukraine. They spoke of God's miraculous intervention to help them escape during the war. They were courageous and anxious to return to Ukraine to help the people rebuild and to encourage them with the Gospel. As we prayed with them, there was no fear in their eyes, just a burning to continue the work God had called them to complete. They have returned as ambassadors to Ukraine with our love, prayers, and blessings. They have a calling and an assignment on their lives to Ukraine. They know the calling may be unto death. They go fearlessly. Their faith overcomes their fear. They have an assignment, and they know it will not be complete unless they go.

We are to be kingdom runners. Your future wants you to run with your gift. You will find breakthroughs while you are running. Your future needs greater hunger and passion like Elijah and Elisha. Elisha followed Elijah and plowed the field until it was time for Elijah to give Elisha his mantle (see 2 Kgs. 2, NIV). You plow the field where God has placed you, and He will place His mantle on you. Where you don't feel the presence of God, you take His presence. Seek after God and His anointing power. We are ambassadors representing Him. Where have you been called to take the gospel?

Your future needs you to never stop contending for the faith. The faithful stand out from the crowd. You don't have the luxury to quit. There is something inside of you the nations need. Your anointing is not unto repentance. Go after God. Carry revival, operating in signs, wonders, and power. What have you done lately? Have you turned your world upside down for the cause of Jesus Christ?

As ambassadors we are to walk humbly with our God. Humility is a graceful confidence that emanates when our trust is in the One whom we believe. It is through humility that we can touch the hearts of others. It is the ordinary things people do daily that makes an extraordinary difference in the lives of others. With humble hearts, we have influence. There are missionaries who take the gospel to places where they know they may be killed for sharing the gospel. They are ready to give their lives. They have already surrendered their lives before they go. We should surrender our hearts as we go forth in the harvest fields where we are every day.

We must also have burning hearts that love and are devoted to Him. We are to be in the middle of His grace and carry grace to others, being ambassadors of grace. Plant yourself in the harvest field where God has placed you. We must have a pure relationship with God to have pure relationships with others. We are to maintain burning hearts passionate for others.

God knows the perfect timing for His purpose to be fulfilled. Jesus made provision through His blood shed on the cross. He is the sacrificial lamb who took our place on the altar so that we can now receive forgiveness of sin. We are to humble ourselves before Him in repentance. We open our hearts to His love and true grace found in His forgiveness that brings true, authentic change. God's call is a work of the heart. "His mother said to the servants, do whatever He tells you" (John 2:5, NIV).

Wherever we go, God is with us. "Where can I go from Your Spirit? Where can I flee from Your presence?" (Ps. 139:7, NIV). When God is with you, you know He has your back. Jacob leaned on his staff and blessed his children, and grandchildren. You also have a history to share with the next generation. Put your heart into the future so you can see not only what God is doing now but also see what He has planned in the future. The fire, power, and anointing in you is for the next generation. They need to see the fire in your eyes.

As the wife of a Gideon, I serve as the chaplain for the auxiliary in our area. I have the privilege of praying daily for courageous men and their wives all over the world. These courageous Gideons and their wives answered the call to place Bibles throughout the world. They not only take on the responsibility of giving Bibles, but also testifying of the Gospel of Jesus Christ in churches, prisons, jails, chapels, wherever the doors open. In some countries, these brave men and women share the Gospel through giving Bibles and giving their testimonies at the possible peril of losing their lives. There are some countries that are not open to receiving the Gospel, and these areas are particularly dangerous. Ambassadors of the Gospel and missionaries make the decision to give their lives for the sake of the Gospel before they go. When they are faced with death, they have already given their lives away. When I pray, I always remember that we have martyrs among us, and they are counting on our prayers.

When Covid-19 hit the world, it stopped the Gideons from being able to go into places and take the Gospel and share the Good News. The doors began to open in our area in 2021. Places that had been somewhat resistant in our area at times were open and received the Bibles willingly. At one physician's office, we had asked whether we could leave a Bible in the waiting room and told them we had special testaments for each nurse. As the nurse went into the back area to ask the doctor if they could receive the Bibles, a gentleman, who looked like he was possibly a veteran, asked if we had an extra Bible that he could have. We said, of course, and gave him one. Then other patients in the room asked if they could have a Bible. These precious men and women are ambassadors of the Gospel in the United States and across the world. The harvest is white, and there is a hunger for the gospel.

The disciples received a commission from God that was reaffirmed and expanded in the book of Matthew: "Go therefore and make disciples of all the nations. Baptizing them in the name of the Father and the Son and the Holy Spirit, teaching them to observe all that I commanded you; and lo, I am with you always, even to the end of the age" (Matt. 28:19–20, NIV).

"When a train goes through a tunnel and it gets dark, you don't throw away the ticket and jump off. You sit still and trust the engineer."[28] As ambassadors, we carry the Gospel inside of us and place our trust in the Lord. We are commissioned to take the Gospel to the world. As ambassadors, we are also to walk a life worthy of the calling. We are to live intentionally being students of the Word of God.

Dig a Little Deeper

1. What does it mean to be an ambassador of grace?

_____

_____

_____

2. Where have you been called to take the Gospel?

_____

_____

_____

3. Do you have a testimony of being an ambassador to your world?

_____

_____

_____

Daily Prayer

Lord, lead us in paths of righteousness and may we always keep our eyes on You that we might have influence in the lives of others. May we be ambassadors of Your love. You guide us on this journey, and You make a way when there seems to be no way. Thank you, Lord, for You always take care of us with your power and grace. As we seek to follow You, may we bring honor to You. We ask that Your will be done in our lives. We pray that we may serve You by serving others and that our lives will reflect You and Your character. May we be the hands and feet of Jesus to the world. Amen.

"The Lord is gracious, and full of compassion; slow to anger, and of great mercy" (Ps. 145:8, KJV).

"The Lord bless thee and keep thee: The Lord make his face shine upon thee and be gracious unto thee: The Lord lift up his countenance upon thee and give thee peace" (Num. 6:24–26, KJV).

DAY 20

Simply Grace

G OD'S SIMPLE GRACE makes a way for Him to use us. For a summer, I was a children's music director for the Jewish Community Center. What you need to know is that I am not Jewish. I was clear with the rabbi that I was a Christian. He told me that he felt God would have me to be the music director for that year's summer camp. What you also need to know is that I have limited musical ability. I could play the piano just enough to get by. I had worked with children in my home church, so I knew a lot of children's songs. The songs I knew were all about Jesus. I can only attribute this assignment as God's holy sense of humor and grace.

The rabbi's son and daughter were in my music class. Every day for weeks, I taught them songs about Jesus, the Messiah. They taught me Jewish prayers, and I learned much from the children and my coworkers who were all Jewish. I sat in a class daily that the rabbi taught from the Torah to the older students. I knew this was a gift for me that I treasured deeply. As the rabbi read of the coming Messiah, my heart would leap in me, knowing the Messiah lived in me. I was the only non-Jewish person on the campus. But I still openly shared Jesus with the other leaders my age. I taught the children many songs about the Lord.

It wasn't until the children put on a musical program for their parents that I was chastised by the rabbi to stick to songs that were not about Jesus, for some of the parents had expressed concerns. I told him I in no way meant to offend. So, for the rest of the summer, the music reflected Jewish songs with an explanation from me that as a Christian, I believed that Jesus was the Messiah of whom we sang. The rabbi seemed comfortable with that revision. God gave simple grace so that I could continue to share Jesus the Messiah with these children, my co-workers, and even this rabbi. God amazes me on the lengths He goes to move men's hearts to open doors when our hearts are committed to Him. Before that summer was over, I had shared about Jesus to many of the staff and teachers. I believe seeds were planted in good soil.

One of my favorite scriptures is Psalm 19. I love the part that talks about the ordinances of the Lord are sweeter than honey and the honeycomb. This scripture comes to life with each example that David gave us.

> "The law of the Lord is perfect, reviving the soul. The statues of the Lord are trustworthy, making wise the simple. The precepts of the Lord are right, giving joy to the heart. The commands of the Lord are radiant, giving light to the eyes. The fear of the Lord is pure, enduring forever. The ordinances of the Lord are sure and altogether righteous. They are more precious than gold, than much pure gold; they are sweeter than honey, than honey from the comb. By them is your servant warned; in keeping them is great reward" (Ps. 19:7–11, NIV; emphasis added).

There is a part in this scripture that says the statutes of the Lord make wise the simple. Let's keep it simple. Let's remember our call is about sharing Jesus with others. "Put your hand to the plow and don't look back" (see Luke 9:62, KJV). Don't be distracted by other's emotions, drama, words, actions, or choices. Don't let others keep you from fulfilling your calling and purpose. Don't let others' failure to plan hinder the plan God has for you. *You never know what is behind your 'Yes.' Don't be afraid to step out.*[29]

As we end one season and begin another, there is a process of purging out the old to make room for the new. To glorify God, we must simplify our daily lives, reprioritize, and remove those things that are hindering us from obtaining God's best. As David said in the scripture: "The law of the Lord is perfect, converting the soul: the testimony of the Lord is sure, making wise the simple" (Psalm 19:7, KJV). I have heard it said: "Simplify to glorify."

Abraham was told to move the tent stakes in preparation for enlarging his tent. Sometimes we have so much clutter in our lives that we have no more room in our tents to expand or even find what we need. We are like a cistern being poured into and out. We become stagnate water, polluted, if not poured out consistently. We must also filter that water to preserve the best and keep out the impurities. In our lives, we should be surrounded with those things that are of some significance, which are reminders of God's faithfulness, memorials of his goodness. We need to filter out those things in our lives that are not a part of God's plan for us.

When you have emotional needs, you will either try to fill that emptiness with things or you will empty everything and hold on to nothing. Christ Jesus is the only one who can truly fill the empty places in our lives. We may seek recognition by pouring ourselves into a profession or just some acknowledgment that we are good enough, but mostly we want relationships and to be genuinely loved. Sometimes we try to substitute the recognition from others for what we are not finding in personal relationships. Even those we hold the most precious will disappoint and at times leave us in a state of longing to be loved. Christ alone can fulfill that hungering to be loved, to be genuinely appreciated for the creation He made.

It takes simply having grace in your life, knowing that you are trusting God alone for the fulfillment of His call on your life to take the Gospel to those who don't yet know Him. Refuse to give up. It takes a release of faith, a conscious effort, and great desire to stay on course. It requires passion, commitment, perseverance, and sometimes plain stubbornness to stay focused on the prize and not settle for something less. We see this revealed in Isaiah: "For out of Jerusalem will come a remnant, and out of Mt. Zion a band of survivors. The zeal of the Lord Almighty will accomplish this!" (Isa. 37:32, NIV). Glory to Him, Jehovah, who can do all things that concern you. Never doubt God. To truly simplify our lives to glorify God requires an uncommon grace working in us.

"God, the master Producer and Orchestrator of life, has some surprises in store for us all. He just loves to tell secrets to His own. Throughout history, He has given glimpses of what was to come. As people, we carry a sense of hope that things can and must be better than they are presently. Everything lives under the influence of this inner desire."[30] It is God's uncommon grace in our lives

that enables us to fully live out the life God has created for us to live. As we simplify this life, we find that our purpose is to glorify Him.

Dig a Little Deeper

1. What does it mean to simplify in order to glorify God?

_____

_____

_____

2. What does it take to stay focused on the prize?

_____

_____

_____

3. What does it take to stay the course?

_____

_____

_____

Daily Prayer

Lord, let our daily prayer be that we might simplify our lives to glorify You. Let us keep our minds on You. May our hearts be filled with a desire to please You with our lives. Lord, may we be faithful in following You. Fill us, Lord, with all of You so there is no room for anything else to fill our lives. Lord, we desire to know You and to know Your perfect will for our lives. Help us when we try to fill the empty places in our lives with things that are not of You. Lord, we desire a genuine relationship with You and others. Even when we are disappointed by people, Lord, be that steadfast anchor we need to stay steady and on course. We place our trust in You alone. Amen,

"Therefore, it is of faith that it might be by grace;
to the end the promise might be sure to all the
seed; not that only which is of the law, but to
that also which is of the faith of Abraham; who
is the father of us all" (Rom. 4:16, KJV).

"But God commended his love toward us, in that, while
we were yet sinners, Christ died for us" (Rom. 5:8, KJV).

DAY 21

Grace and Gratitude

WHEN OUR YOUNGEST son, Matthew, was three years old, one night he became very sick. He was having trouble breathing. My husband scooped him up in his arms, and we hurried to the hospital. By the time we arrived at the hospital, Mathew was gasping for air, and he was turning blue. The doctors took him quickly in for an x-ray, and his physician was called. They brought him back to us and showed us the x-ray. His throat and airways looked like someone's hands were on his throat squeezing the life out of him. He was barely getting any air at all, and it appeared they would need to do surgery to open the airways.

Joe had been holding Matthew in his arms and had been singing and praying over Matthew as we waited for the doctors. We needed a miracle for our little boy. I know it was probably only minutes until the surgery team all arrived, but it felt like hours. I was afraid they were going to be too late. We continued to pray. Then Matthew in his dad's arms began to sing the song his dad had been singing over him. "*Oh, the blood of Jesus. Oh, the blood of Jesus, that washes white as snow.*"[31] The doctor, his surgeon, came to Matthew and listened as he sang. She said, "I have seen the x-rays and they tell us to do surgery, but I want to take one more x-ray before we take him in for surgery."

The doctor came out with two x-rays. The first looked like his airways were completely closed. The second showed open airways, and the cloud that had been around his throat was gone. The doctor said, "He will not need surgery. God has healed your little boy. There is no other way to explain it. See, the x-rays tell the story."

They kept Matthew at the hospital overnight for observation, and he and I slept under an oxygen tent. The next day, he was back home, and that Sunday we testified of this miracle before the church. We are so grateful for God's grace and mercy that saved the life of our child yet another time. This miracle was a testimony of God's faithfulness not only to us, but also to the medical team.

We knew God had saved Matthew for a purpose. Little did we know that he would one day be a pediatrician, saving the lives of other little children. When Matthew was completing his residency in Arkansas, he was, at times, working in the Neonatal Intensive Care Unit. I asked him how hard it was for him working with these babies in crisis and how he was handling it when one of these little ones didn't survive. His response was "not on my watch." He wasn't being prideful, just the opposite. He knew how hard it was to keep those babies alive. His words were a declaration that he was doing everything to make sure they survived.

When we have done all we know to do, God makes our impossible possible. Even if you don't receive your miracle, God's grace is enough to see you through. Gratitude turns what we have into enough—and more. It turns denial into acceptance, chaos into order, and confusion into clarity. It makes sense of our past, brings peace for today, and creates a vision for tomorrow.

The story of Mary and Martha is a story about making dead things come to life. Mary and Martha called for Jesus to come and heal their brother, Lazarus, in Bethany. Jesus did not come until after Lazarus had died. It was believed that the soul leaves the body on the third day. It was on the fourth day when Jesus showed up and called Lazarus back to life. This is known as a fourth-day miracle. Death was swallowed up in victory. Jesus was the Grave Robber. Jesus overcame death by calling Lazarus out of the tomb four days after he was dead. This is known as one of Jesus's greatest miracles, as His words brought life. They thought it was too late for a miracle, but Jesus was right on time. Jesus understood Mary and Martha's grief. He showed compassion and grace by bringing about this miracle (see John 11, NIV).

You may think it is too late for you to receive your miracle. God is never late. He is always on time. *In the waiting, the meantime, the in-between time, it all serves a purpose. Trust your process even the delays and detours. Never doubt. He is working. He is changing lives. He will cause all your waiting to be used for His purpose.*[32] It is during these times you have been given this great opportunity for God to work on you on the inside developing patience as you persevere.

We live a transformed life. God's Word leads us to be conformed to our Creator. God's grace brings peace, joy, and everlasting love. Grace changes us. You were created to serve as Martha exemplified. You were also created for worship as Mary exemplified. Servanthood does not live for the applause of others. We live for an audience of one. If you want the extraordinary, try serving in ordinary ways.

We are to approach the throne of grace with confidence and find mercy and grace in a time of need. God gives us a future beyond our past. Prayer is where the natural ends and the supernatural begins. "Then touched He the man's eyes, saying, 'According to your faith be it unto you'" (Matthew 9:29, KJV). And the man was healed. That day, he received sight and vision from the Messiah, God is looking for hearts burning for Him and walking in His sovereign grace. As we dwell in His presence through our daily walk, we grow in His love and compassion for a dying world. We are sanctified by the truth we find in His Word. We are filled with gratitude for God's grace in our lives.

Unmerited grace was given to Joseph's brothers when they had set out to kill him, but Joseph's ultimate response was to save them. We see unmerited favor also with David in the cave with King Saul. He could have killed him, but instead, he simply cut off a piece of his garment. We can see by their behavior; David was already walking in his destiny to be king and Joseph as the Leader over all of Egypt. We see this unmerited grace throughout the scriptures, as in Colossians 3:16–17:

> "Let the Word of Christ dwell in you richly as you teach and admonish one another with all wisdom, and as you sing psalms, hymns, and spiritual songs with gratitude in your hearts to God. And whatever you do, whether in word or deed, do it all in the name of the Lord Jesus, giving thanks to God the Father through Him."

Grace and truth produce anointing to the humble, and a spirit of grace and supplication produce a testimony of strength and humility (see Prov.

3:34, NIV). "You are the most excellent of men and your lips have been anointed with grace, since God has blessed you forever" (Ps. 45:2, NIV).

Dig a Little Deeper

1. What does it mean that we are sanctified by the truth that we find in His Word?

_____

_____

_____

2. Explain how grace and truth bring anointing.

_____

_____

_____

3. What is meant by: If you want the extraordinary in your life, try serving in ordinary ways?

_____

_____

_____

Daily Prayer

Lord, let our daily prayer be that we will walk in grace and dependence on You to give us the strength and revelation to walk out our destiny. May we always keep our hearts and minds in remembrance of the sacrifice Jesus made for us with grateful hearts. Lord, give us strength and humility to live a life of grace and gratitude. Amen.

"And the child grew, and waxed strong in spirit, filled with wisdom: and the grace of God was upon him" (Luke 2:40, KJV).

"And therefore, will the Lord wait, that He may be gracious unto you, and therefore will He be exalted, that He may have mercy upon you; for the Lord is a God of judgment: blessed are all they that wait for Him" (Isa. 30:18, KJV).

DAY 22

Amazing Grace

WHEN IN ROME, we found the Mamertine prison that is thought to be the place Paul was imprisoned for the second time. It was a cave just north of the Roman Forum. There were times that sewage would back up into the cave. It is thought that Paul wrote the book of Philippians while in these circumstances. It was in this place that Paul wrote to the church at Philippi saying, "I am not saying this because I am in need, for I have learned to be content whatever the circumstances" (Phil. 4:11, NIV). It takes amazing grace to be content with the Lord no matter the circumstances.

Grace is indeed amazing. It transforms sinners into saints; it overcomes the power of sin and sets people free. Grace is an undeserved favor. When we come to Christ, we are given the gift of God's grace. We see God's gift of grace in the scriptures: "For all have sinned and fall short of the glory of God, and are justified freely by His grace, through the redemption that came by Christ Jesus" (Rom. 3:23–24, NIV). Grace is a precious gift available to us only through the blood of Christ. Jesus paid the price; we need only accept the gift.

> "Amazing grace! How sweet the sound, that saved a wretch like me! I once was lost, but now am found, was blind, but now I see."[33]

Recently we stood in the Colosseum in Rome, where it is believed that Christians fought for their lives while entertaining crowds. Standing there, looking around at the theater, it was overwhelming to think of the sacrifice they made for the sake of the Gospel of Jesus Christ. I was reminded of Peter's sacrifice, as legend has recorded, that he chose to return to Rome where he was hung upside down on a cross. He made a choice to be martyred.

We walked through the catacombs and saw where many Christians had been buried. In Ancient Rome, it was not permitted for bodies to be buried inside the city walls, so the Christians built these underground cemeteries. I recently visited a newly discovered burial ground in Rome. They would bury three children together next to a small cave area. It was hot above the ground. But as we descended into the catacombs, it became cool. There were long stairways reaching far beneath the earth. There were many rows of covered bodies. It would have been easy to get lost among the graves. The early church met in those catacombs. It was amazing grace that kept them safe as they gathered.

Until we experience grace in the deepest recesses of our hearts and minds and realize its all-encompassing power over our lives, we won't really understand it. For when God opens our eyes to our utter dependence on His love and compassion, we are suddenly released to love others.

We must purpose to have an abundance of His grace, mentally transforming our minds, spiritually and physically transforming our hearts. May an abundance of grace strengthen us and guard us from all that may come against us. It is in His grace; we find His goodness. We must purpose to access His abundant grace for every need and every circumstance. Great is His faithfulness to provide grace to be applied to every aspect of our lives. Paul preached about this amazing grace. "Many of the Jews and devout converts of Judaism followed Paul and Barnabas, who, as they spoke with them, urged them to continue in the grace of God" (Acts 13:43, ESV). God bestows on us an overwhelming abundance of grace.

Through God's amazing grace, Paul continued to preach the Gospel bringing God's amazing grace to the world. "So, they remained for a long time, speaking boldly for the Lord, who bore witness to the world of His grace, granting signs and wonders to be done by their hands" (Acts 14:3, ESV). "Paul chose Silas and departed, having been commended by the brothers to the grace of the Lord" (Acts 15:40, ESV). "And when he wished to cross to Achaia, the brothers encouraged him and wrote to the disciples to welcome him. When he arrived, he greatly helped those who through grace had believed" (Acts 18:27, ESV).

> *We are containers that carry the Holy Spirit. We are a light in the darkness. Neuma (sic) in the Greek means presence, spirit, breath, Spirit of God. Paraclete in the Greek is one who comes beside you as the comforter. We are the people of God, that remnant that still believes and clings to Jesus Christ and have His spirit burning inside of us.* [34]

The scriptures tell us that we are God's remnant. "So too, at the present time there is a remnant chosen by grace" (Rom. 11:5, NIV). We cannot within our own selves, our own abilities and giftings, fulfill the assignment He has placed on our lives. He must reside within us, leading us, and providing all we need to fulfill His purpose for us on this earth. We must know Him. We must have an intimate relationship with Him. This requires a willingness on our part to invite Him into every part of our lives. We are called to follow Him as the early church exemplified.

We see in the scriptures that God's amazing grace makes a way for us to have faith and relationship with God. "Therefore, since we have been justified by faith, we have peace with God through our Lord Jesus Christ. Through Him we have obtained access by faith into this grace in which we stand, and we rejoice in hope of the glory of God" (Romans 5:1–2, NIV). God's amazing grace empowered the early Christians, common men and women, to live uncommon, extraordinary lives. Paul tells us in the scriptures of how we are to follow Jesus and His ways:

> "Paul a servant of Jesus Christ, called to be an apostle, separated unto the gospel of God, concerning his Son Jesus Christ our Lord which was made of the seed of David according to the flesh; And declared to be the Son of God with power, according to the spirit of holiness, by the resurrection from the dead: By whom we have received grace and

apostleship, for obedience to the faith among all nations, for his name" (Rom. 1:1–5, KJV).

God loves us, and He will not leave us. God is good even when the circumstances are darker than you ever imagined. God is good even when people are not. God is good even when things seem hopeless. When we can't hear His voice, we must trust His heart. When you come to the end of you, you find Him. It is His amazing grace that sustains us daily. It is this grace that restores, renews, refines, and revives us.

Dig a Little Deeper

1. Tell how amazing grace empowered the early church.

    _____

    _____

    _____

2. What does the scripture mean when it says that we are a remnant chosen by grace?

    _____

    _____

    _____

3. What does it mean to follow Jesus and His ways?

_____

_____

_____

Daily Prayer

Lord, let our daily prayer be that we are transformed by Your amazing grace. May Your undeserved favor on us enable us to live a life that brings hope and light to others. Thank you for the gift of Your amazing grace. You have brought us on this journey of grace. Thank you, Lord, for the way You always sustain us with Your power, and You guide us through each trial we encounter. You are so faithful, God. You draw us near to You, and You embrace us with Your loving kindness. We seek You and all You are. May we grow ever closer to You and show forth Your amazing grace to this world. Amen.

"But they that wait upon the Lord shall renew their strength; they shall mount up with wings as eagles; they shall run, and not be weary, and they shall walk, and not faint" (Isa. 40:31, KJV).

"But God, who is rich in mercy, for His great love wherewith He loved us, even when we were dead in sins, hath quickened us together with Christ, by grace ye are saved" (Eph. 2:4–5, KJV).

DAY 23

Everlasting Grace

G OD GIVES US a future beyond our past. He brings an everlasting grace into our lives. Jesus came from the lineage of five scandalous women: Tamar, Ruth, Rahab, Mary mother of Jesus, and Bathsheba. These women were important on purpose. Their lives are stories of redemption that eventually led through Jesus's lineage to the ultimate redemption found in Jesus. These women had both passion and a testimony of redemption.

Tamar the daughter in law of Judah who was of the lineage of Jesus was found to be in a scandalous situation. Tamar's husband, Er, was evil in the sight of the Lord. God killed him. Judah sent his second born son Onan to marry Tamar to be with her to have a child, but Onan did not obey the Lord, so he was also killed. Tamar set herself up as a prostitute and tricked Judah to having sexual relations with her, and she became pregnant. Tamar had lived through the deaths of her husbands. She set herself up for scandal by tricking Judah. Despite what she had to go through, God still triumphed in her life and used her to be in the genealogy of Jesus. Her ultimate redemption came through the Messiah (see Gen. 38:1–30; Matt. 1:3, NIV).

Rahab wanted a piece of the calling. Rahab was a harlot and Gentile from Jericho living on the wall. She chose to help Joshua and Caleb, the Israelite spies. She helped make a way for the Israelites to come in from the wilderness and take the land. Because she helped them, God provided a way for her family to escape the impending destruction of Jericho. She was the least of the least. Everything about her would be considered unclean. Because of her choice to help the Israelites, she and her household were spared. She was of the ancestry and lineage of King David and Jesus (see Josh. 2:1–21, NIV). You decide what your calling is and do it, just as Rahab did (see Josh. 6:22–25, NIV).

Mary, the mother of Jesus brought scandal into her life when she chose to be trusted with the Godchild, Jesus. However, Mary also found favor with God. (Luke 1:30, NIV) Jesus grew up in Nazareth, a small area. Jesus had a humble, scandalous beginning, as He was born of a woman who was pregnant out of wedlock. Jesus was rejected by the Jews, for whom He had come to earth and had taken on humanity, to bring redemption. He died on a cross that was next to the side of a busy road, naked and disgraced. He was made a mockery of and an example of what could happen to you if you acted and spoke as He did. Jesus ate with tax collectors and prostitutes. He spent time with fishermen, and He showed compassion to widows and Gentiles. He welcomed the lepers and insane. "Blessed is she who has believed that the Lord would fulfill His promises to her!" (Luke 1:45, NIV). "To proclaim the year of the Lord's favor" (Luke 4:19, NIV). Mary was a model of surrender to the will of God. She gave up everything she was expecting from life to follow the calling of God. We see everlasting grace, as we see Mary yield her life to God.

Ruth came from Moab, a heathen land. When her husband died, she followed her mother-in-law to her homeland, Bethlehem. She was the great-grandmother of King David and named in the genealogy of Jesus. This begins the redemption story paralleling or foreshadowing the redemption story of Jesus who came from Bethlehem of Judea. Most of the story is set in the Harvest Fields. However, Ruth was also brought to this humble place of scandal when she chose to lay on the threshing floor at Boaz's feet through the night. Even though this was a part of the covenant and law for Boaz to take Ruth after the other relative did not take her; the visual presented of her being with Boaz at night at his feet and awakening him during the night appeared scandalous. However, Ruth's redemption came through her kinsmen redeemer, Boaz, when he married her. Everlasting grace comes to us through our Kinsmen Redeemer, Jesus (see Ruth, chapters 1 and 2).

Bathsheba is probably the most scandalous one on this list. It was so much so that Matthew couldn't even bring himself to put her name in the genealogy. He refers to her as the wife of Uriah. She had an adulterous relationship with King David, and it nearly destroyed him. David took her, and she ended up pregnant, bringing shame on her, and then the king had her husband sent to the front lines in war to be killed. Mosaic law said that Bathsheba and David should have been stoned to death. David and Bathsheba felt the trauma of losing their child soon after birth. We have a woman who, by every right, could claim to be broken and cursed. Yet her story did not end there.

Once David had reconciled with God, he married Bathsheba and they had another son, Solomon. Bathsheba was inspirational in that she did not dwell in the label of adulterous and sinner. Instead, she found forgiveness and moved forward so powerfully that her son became king and is still regarded as the wisest man to walk the earth except for Jesus. Their child then became a part of the lineage of Jesus. Redemption came through Jesus even through this lineage (see 2 Sam. 11:1–5; 12:24–25; Matt. 1:6, NIV).

Many of the things we go through are setting us up for our purpose. God opens doors and sends you out at the right time and makes provision for the vision. God has a divine purpose for your life. The spirit of God arouses us from within. Waiting does not diminish us. The longer the wait, the longer we become more joyful over the expectancy. We have been enlarged, pregnant with purpose (see Rom. 8:22–25, ESV). The Holy Ghost functions like the archer pulling back the arrow. You have been pulled back, ready to be sent forth for purpose. As we have seen in the lives of these five scandalous women, in their weakness, He was made strong. Even though they had been through immense challenges, God was faithful.

God's everlasting grace embraces the broken and restores their royal crowns on his daughters. Even when we go through the depths of shame, He reaches out to where we are to pull us up and set our feet on solid ground. You were made on purpose for a purpose. "I will praise you, for I am fearfully and wonderfully made; Marvelous are your works, and that my soul knows very well" (Ps. 139:14, NKJV Spirit-filled Life Bible). God's grace sees you through your pain and makes purpose out of your pain.

Dig a Little Deeper

1. Can you think of a time when you went through a situation that was a set up for God's ultimate plan for you?

_____

_____

_____

2. What does it mean that God is like an archer pulling back on the bow?

_____

_____

_____

3. What does it mean to be pregnant with purpose?

_____

_____

_____

Daily Prayer

Jesus, break our hearts with what breaks Yours. Let us not be limited by our past. May we wholeheartedly pursue You and Your purpose in our lives. May Your everlasting grace be with us and in us throughout our lives. The storm is temporary, but you, Lord, are eternal. You have been faithful through the ages. We put our trust in You. Lord God, You are with us. You are the mighty Warrior who saves. You take the broken and scandalous and restore their crowns. Amen.

"Let your speech be always with grace, seasoned
with salt, that ye may know how ye ought
to answer every man" (Col. 4:6, KJV).

"He hath not dealt with us after our sins; nor
rewarded us according to our iniquities. For as the
heaven is high above the earth, so great is his mercy
toward them that fear him" (Ps. 103:10–11, KJV).

DAY 24

Divine Grace

W HILE TRAVELING IN Italy, my husband and I discovered a place called Matera, found in the southernmost part of Italy. There is an area in Matera known as the Sassi-di-Matera, which is a complex of cave dwellings carved into the ancient river canyon. Matera is believed to have been settled since the tenth millennium BC. This makes it potentially one of the oldest continually inhabited settlements in the world; it is the oldest city in Europe. During the reign of Nero, many Christians fled Rome to Matera. They lived in the caves of the Sassi, and even today, you can see many Christian frescos (drawings) on the walls of the caves in Matera. People from many different cultures, including Jews, have settled there as they have fled oppression. It was divine grace that hid these people from the Roman armies chasing after them.

When Nero was burning Christians to light up his garden and Christians were being martyred, some were able to escape persecution by fleeing to Matera. Because Matera was known to be such a distance from Rome and had been known as a poor area, the soldiers didn't pursue the Christians as far as Matera. Today, Matera is filled with Christians and other cultures, who are descendants from that period of persecution. We were able to see the lights coming from the caves of the homes and businesses at night. During the day, we were able to go into the businesses and homes of the cave dwellers. As we walked through the different areas, we could see the many different cultures that had settled there and had been rescued by literally living in the cleft of the rock. Those who fled to this area were protected by God's divine grace. This is where *The Passion of the Christ* was filmed.

God brought Joseph from the pit to the palace. He will bring you out of your pit and place you in the purpose He has for your life as you trust in Him (see Gen. Chapters 37–50). Joseph reassured his brothers that although they plotted evil against him, God transformed their evil for His divine plan and purpose to save a family and a nation. Despite years of unjust suffering, Joseph neither harbored unforgiveness nor succumbed to bitterness and resentment. Instead, he exhibited great love and kindness toward his brothers. God's divine grace was seen in Joseph as he forgave his family. This spiritual grace is not self-produced; it arises as we yield to the Spirit's release of forgiving love in our hearts. The Psalmist best expresses this spiritual grace this way: "Show me Your ways, Oh Lord, teach me Your paths; guide me in Your truth and teach me, for You are God my Savior, and my hope is in You all day long" (Ps. 25:4–5, NIV). He is a faithful God. He desires that we would always be full of faith in a trusting relationship with Him, no matter the circumstances.

Samuel anointed David (see 1 Sam., chapters 16 and 17). This was the first of three anointings David experienced. The second was as king over Judah, and the third anointing was as king over Israel. David's potential was solidified on the shepherd's field. It was the lion and the bear that prepared him for the giant. We go through difficult and challenging times to prepare us to defeat the giants in our lives. David said to the giant, "I come to you in the name of the Lord of hosts, the God of the armies of Israel; this is the day the Lord will deliver you into my hand" (see 1 Sam. 17).

David was anointed and then placed in position. Be content where you are until God moves you to another place. He is called the God of grace. This is a powerful promise that He Himself will restore you. We are to be faithful as God is faithful to us. "And the God of all grace, called you to His eternal glory in Christ, after you have suffered a little while, will Himself restore you and make you strong, firm and steadfast" (1 Pet. 5:10, NIV).

We see in Genesis how God provided for Abraham. God provided the sacrifice at just the right moment that was needed to spare Abraham's son. "Abraham looked up, and there in the thicket, he saw a ram caught by its horns. And he went over and took the ram and sacrificed it as a burnt offering instead of his son. So, Abraham called that place 'The Lord will Provide.' And to this day it is said that on the mountain of the Lord it will be provided" (Gen. 22:13–14, NIV). We receive God's provisions in God's timing.

Corrie ten Boom once spoke of her father telling her, "*God gives you the ticket for the train just as it is time to board. You do not need the ticket until it is the right time*" *(1900)*.

In Psalm 89, we see how God is always going before us to make the way for us. "Righteousness and justice are the foundation of Your throne; love and faithfulness go before You" (Ps. 89:14, NIV). When you are going through a challenge, keep hope and courage. Don't quit. Stick with the basics you know to be truth. When we are tested in our faith, we are to walk in faith. Be faithful in your covenant to God to trust Him in all circumstances. God's vision is unveiled to you to bring the lost to God. He calls you, then gifts you to share the saving grace of Jesus. You are to walk out the vision God has for your life. "For it is God who works in you to will and to act according to His good purpose" (Phil. 2:13, NIV). When we desire to do what pleases Him, He gives us the power to do it through His divine grace. However, we must work it out, so pick up your cross. The purposes of God will prevail in your life. Jesus is I Am that I Am. Love God, love others, and walk in His precepts. Seek first the kingdom of God. This is walking out your faith with divine grace.

"Love and faithfulness meet together; righteousness and peace kiss each other. Faithfulness springs forth from the earth, and righteousness looks down from heaven" (Ps. 85:10–11, NIV). "Because of the Lord's great love, we are not consumed, for His compassions never fail, they are new every morning; great is your faithfulness" (Lam. 3:22–23, NIV). Out of the test comes our testimony. "God has a reason for allowing things to happen. We may never understand His wisdom, but we simply have to trust His will" (Ps. 37:5, NIV).

Failure doesn't negate what you are called to do. Never give up or give in. If God has placed a desire within you, given you a task or talent, or called you to something, start where you are. Be intentional at the place you are at now. God will empower you where you are for the task He has called you. Step out of your comfort zone. God's divine grace will empower you to fulfill whatever God has called you to do. His divine grace enables you to walk out a godly life and follow God with all your heart.

Dig a Little Deeper

1. We see God's divine purpose unfold in Joseph's life as God brought him from the pit to the palace. Can you remember a time that God brought you through a time of devastation and then revealed his favor and purpose in your life?

_____

_____

_____

2. Divine grace is grace that occurs at the hand of God. Can you remember a time that God brought you through and you knew you would not have made it through if it had not been for the grace of God?

_____

_____

_____

3. Can you think of a time in your life when your faith was challenged? How did you make it through this time?

_____

_____

_____

Daily Prayer

Father, may our daily prayer be that we will seek Your ways, walk in Your paths, be guided in truth, that we will learn of You and place our hope in You that we may be stable, secure, and faithful as You are faithful toward us. May we draw close to know You, love You, and share Your love with others. Lord, increase our faith. Keep our eyes on You, depending on You, Lord, to always be our Way Maker. Your divine grace brings miracles and increases our faith in You. Despite our weaknesses, You are strong, and You always make a way when there seems to be no way. Thank you, Lord, for making what seemed impossible, possible. My trust is in You. Amen.

"The Lord is a refuge for the oppressed, a stronghold in times of trouble. Those who know Your name will trust in You. For You, Lord, have never forsaken those who seek You" (Ps. 9:9–10, NIV).

"And Stephen, full of faith and power, did great wonders and miracles among the people" (Acts 6:8, KJV).

DAY 25

Saving Grace

I F NOT FOR the saving grace of God, where would I be? Where would you be? How different our lives would have been without the saving grace of Jesus Christ! I remember the night, the moment, I came to the saving knowledge of Jesus. I grew up with Christian parents, attended church, and had Christian friends; but that night I knew in my heart that I did not have a personal relationship with Jesus. Only you can determine in your heart whether you have experienced His saving grace for you personally.

I was only ten years old; I had gone to church with a friend. It was the last night of the revival when the pastor preached a fiery sermon on heaven and hell and of God's great love and the sacrifice of Jesus, His son. I could feel my heart beating so fast. I knew this was my moment. Somehow, I knew this moment would change my life forever. I was afraid to go to the front of the church to answer the call to follow Jesus. Fear has always been my greatest enemy. My hands clinched the pew in front of me. The music stopped. The service was over.

I had a sickening feeling in my gut that I had missed my opportunity to come to know my Savior. I was small, and the adults around me seemed ten feet tall. I squeezed in between the crowd and made my way to the preacher. I was shaking; I was so afraid I had missed my moment. I tugged on his jacket, and he looked down to see who was pulling on him. He leaned down, and I whispered in his ear, "Am I too late? Is it too late for me to be saved?" He knelt beside me and said, "It is never too late to come to know the Lord." He prayed with me, and I asked Jesus to come into my heart.

I knew instantly that my life had been changed forever. I felt an overwhelming love that filled every part of me, and I knew that He would be with me forever. I wanted to tell everyone about His saving grace. Your experience may have been different than mine, but you know in your heart if you have come to know His perfect love that has washed away your sins, as only He can. If you haven't come to know His saving grace, I pray that today will be your day.

John the Baptist understood this saving grace. John the Baptist knew Jesus as the Savior for the world and proclaimed His grace saying! "The next day John saw Jesus coming toward him and said, 'Look, the Lamb of God, who takes away the sin of the world!'" (John 1:29, NIV). When John the Baptist called Jesus the Lamb of God, he was talking about the Jewish law requiring an unblemished lamb to be sacrificed for the sins of humanity. Jesus, through the sacrifice of his life, took the place of the sacrificial lamb. Jesus was an uncommon man born in common, ordinary surroundings, with an uncommon call on his life.

He would appear on the scene in the little town of Bethlehem and grew up in the small village of Nazareth. Jesus was no ordinary man. Everything about Him was extraordinary. He was destined to change the world. In what seemed just a common ordinary man resided God Himself. We as the sons and daughters of God are called to carry to the world this same supernatural power that Jesus carried to the world. Jesus brought saving grace through the sacrifice of His life that we might know His saving grace in our lives. God's love for us is so powerful, that while we were still in our sins, He forgave us and drew us to Him. "For God so loved the world, that He gave His one and only Son that whoever believes in Him shall not perish but have eternal life." (John 3:16, NIV)

God is also in what seems common or ordinary, and with His grace, He turns common to uncommon and ordinary to extraordinary. Three of our grandchildren have given their hearts to the Lord over the past two years. London, our oldest grandson, age eleven, had been led to the Lord by his mother and was baptized by his father and pastor. During our recent Fourth of July barbeque, my grandson, Levi, age seven, shared that he had given his heart to Jesus that week. His mother shared with the family that Levi was at the YMCA gym, and he began asking her questions about how Jesus could be in your heart and how he could be saved. God had been speaking to him and moving in his heart preparing him for this moment. My precious daughter-in-law led him in prayer, and he asked Jesus to be his Savior. He had shared this at church, with family and friends.

My granddaughter, Everly, age six, quickly also shared with the family gathered around the table that she, too, had asked Jesus to be her Savior. Her mother had also led Everly into a prayer for salvation. There is no greater thing a mother can do than lead her children to know Jesus. These two mothers have been living such exemplary lives that their children knew to come to them and be led to the Savior. Leading your children to the Lord is truly one of the most extraordinary things you will ever do.

The plan for your life far exceeds the circumstances of your day. "The Lord directs the steps of the godly" (see Ps. 37:23–24, NIV). Know your purpose. Purpose to live on purpose. If you have a dream in your heart, hear this: "In all your ways acknowledge Him and He will direct thy paths" (Prov. 3:6, KJV). Keep dreaming with God! Don't let fear take your moment away. Move on from yesterday. God is already in your tomorrow.

When in Israel we stood looking across at Golgotha, where a busy road and marketplace had once been. Among the great crowds, Jesus was humiliated, stripped of His clothes and all decency. He had been beaten, whipped, bloodied, and bruised. He was hung on the cross as a common thief (see Matt. 26, KJV), although there was nothing common about Him. He shed His blood and gave His life that we might have eternal life. He is the most extraordinary man to have ever lived upon this earth. God, Himself, came down to earth to take on our sins and provide a way of redemption for us. He was dead and buried, but He arose on the third day, and our Redeemer lives today. The chief priests, scribes, and elders mocked Him while He was on the cross by saying, "He saved others; Himself He cannot save. If He be the King of Israel, let Him now come down from the cross, and we will believe Him" (Matt. 27:42–43, KJV). He chose not to save Himself but decided to sacrifice Himself to provide us His saving grace.

God's saving grace is free for all who will receive Him. We must place our trust in Him. He will make a way for us, and He will direct our paths. We must trust in Him and rely on Him. His saving grace is abundant, and

He is waiting for the lost to come to Him. He is also waiting for us to give our consent to take Him, His Word, to those who don't know Him. May our hearts be "*I have decided to follow Jesus, though none go with me still I will follow.*"[35]

Dig a Little Deeper

1. While we were still in our sins, Jesus came to forgive us and bring salvation to us. Do you have confidence that Jesus is your Savior and the Lord of your life?

_____

_____

_____

2 Can you think of a time God intervened in your life and changed the ordinary to extraordinary?

_____

_____

_____

3   Can you share a time you carried the Gospel to someone, and they came to know the saving grace of Jesus Christ?

_____

_____

_____

Daily Prayer

May our daily prayer be, Father, that we will come to know Your saving grace in our lives. Just as I am, I come to Thee. May we know You and Your saving grace as we walk daily with You. Lord, pour boldness and wisdom in us to share Your Gospel of Good News to others. May we be witnesses to those You place in our paths. Lord, we pray for open doors that we might share You with others. Make the crooked paths straight and go before us so we may be light and salt to others. Amen.

"Now to him that worketh is the reward not reckoned of grace, but of debt. But to him that worketh not, but believeth on Him that justifies the ungodly, his faith is counted for righteousness" (Rom. 4:4–5, KJV).

"Do not be carried away by all kinds of strange teachings. It is good for our hearts to be strengthened by grace, not by eating ceremonial foods, which is of no benefit to those who do so" (Heb. 13:9, NIV).

DAY 26

Sacrificial Grace

J ESUS MADE THE ultimate sacrifice for us through the giving of His life that we might have eternal life. Sacrificial grace requires giving of yourself, your time, your giftings, your abilities, your finances, and sometimes putting your dreams on hold as you meet the needs of others. Volunteers are some of the most unselfish people I have ever known. They often work behind the scenes and rarely receive recognition. I am reminded of the compassion and selflessness of volunteers when I see someone in a Santa Suit ringing a bell, calling us to give to the Salvation Army.

Volunteers can do big things like Doctors without Borders, Franklin Graham's Samaritan's Purse, or Remote Area Medical (RAM) clinics. There are also numerous medical mission groups that set up clinics throughout the world, giving of their time and abilities to help others. There are many churches and agencies that provide assistance through pregnancy centers, food banks, providing clothing, safe housing, and medical services, including vision services at no cost. These volunteers, churches, and agencies often provide services without any acknowledgments. Volunteering is at the heart of sacrificial grace. What are you willing to do? What has God placed in your hand? Are you willing to give?

God called Gideon a "mighty man of valor" before Gideon had stepped into his destiny. Gideon saw himself as the least. However, God will not put you in a place for which you are not prepared. When you listen to God's voice and follow His directions as Gideon did, you will be successful. Gideon was told to bring the men to the water and test them. Gideon was looking for the men who, while they were drinking water, were also watchful (see Judg. 6:11–16; 7:3–4, NIV). Be sober concerning your enemy. Gideon was looking for whom he could trust. God has already delivered your enemy into your hands. In Gideon's situation, the enemy turned on each other. God will give you a strategic plan. Gideon walked in grace, and he sought out the men willing to make the sacrifice to become "mighty men of valor."

Humility and faith were great elements of Gideon's ultimate character. This is the standard that we are to pursue as we spread the Gospel and bring others to the saving knowledge of Jesus Christ. "I waited patiently for the Lord; And He inclined unto me and heard my cry. He brought me up also out of a horrible pit, out of the miry clay, and set my feet upon a rock, and established my steps" (Ps. 40:1–2, KJV).

In Corinthians chapter 12, Paul had a vision, and he pleaded with God three times to take away the thorn in his flesh. God's response to Paul was, "My grace is sufficient for you, for My power is made perfect in weakness." Paul's response was, "Therefore, I will boast all the more gladly about my weaknesses, so that Christ's power may rest on me." May we all know that God's power is greater than our weaknesses, and His grace is sufficient.

We see in the Book of Esther (Esther 1:10-12, NKJV), Queen Vashti was commanded by King Ahasuerus to come before him wearing her royal crown to show her beauty to the people and officials. But Queen Vashti refused the king's command. So, a decree went out that Vashti would no longer come before the king, but another would take her position as queen (See Esther 1:19, NKJV). At the king's request, beautiful young virgins were brought to Shushan, and beauty preparations were given to them. "Mordecai had brought up Hadassah, that is, Esther, his uncle's daughter, for she had neither mother nor father. The young woman was lovely and beautiful. When her father and mother died, Mordecai took her as his own daughter" (Esther 2:7, NKJV). Esther was taken to the king's palace into the care of Hegai. Esther gained favor with Hegai and was given beauty preparations, besides her allowance. Then she was given seven choice maidservants and was moved to the best place in the house. Esther had not revealed her people or family as Mordecai had told her not to reveal.

After the twelve months of preparation required for all the young women, Esther was called to go in before the king. She took with her only what was recommended by Hegai. "The king loved Esther more than all the other women, and she obtained grace and favor in his sight more than all the virgins; so, he set the royal crown upon her head and made her queen instead of Vashti." (Esther 2:17, NJKV).

Mordecai sat within the king's gates. He overheard a plot to kill the king. He told Esther of the plot. She revealed the plot to the king in Mordecai's name. Both the men were hanged on the gallows. Haman was promoted and all the people would bow to him, except for Mordecai. Haman sought to destroy all the Jews including Mordecai. Haman convinced King Ahasuerus that the Jews were not following the king's laws. So, the king gave Haman his signet ring and gave Haman authority to do as he pleased to these people. Haman was determined to kill the Jewish people. Mordecai tore his clothes and put on sackcloth and ashes. The Jews prayed, fasted, weeping and wailing in sackcloth and ashes. There was great mourning among the Jews.

Esther told Mordecai that she could not go before the king without him calling for her or she might die. Mordecai's answer was: "Do not think in your heart that you will escape in the king's palace and more than all the other Jews. For if you remain completely silent at this time, relief and deliverance will arise from another place, but you and your father's house will perish. Yet who knows whether you have come to the kingdom for such a time as this?" (Esther 4:13-14, NKJV).

Esther had a heart that could hear and understand God's plan to use her to bring deliverance. She listened closely to God's instructions and His strategic plan for her. Esther stood in the inner court yards of the king and found favor with the king.

Esther went before the King and requested to make a banquet for the King and Haman. When the first banquet was finished the king asked Esther what is your petition? Esther asked for the King and Haman to come to another banquet she would prepare for them. Haman had gallows made for he was angered by Mordecai. However, the King had read in the records of chronicles and Mordecai had not been rewarded for saving the king's life. So, he had Haman take the robe and the horse, arrayed Mordecai and led him on horseback through the city. At the end of the second banquet the King asked Esther what was her petition? She asked that her life and her people's lives be spared. The King asked who had the heart to do such a thing? Esther answered, "Haman." The king ordered Haman to be hung on the gallows he had prepared for Mordecai. Esther and her people were spared. God gave Esther sacrificial grace, a willingness to give herself for her people.

What is ordinary to us is extraordinary to God. God is with us. We are His daughters. May our story be all about telling His story. We don't deserve the grace that God extends to us. We can't work for it; it is not something we can earn. He gives it freely to all who ask.

Dig a Little Deeper

1. Describe your understanding of sacrificial grace.

_____

_____

_____

2. Explain what it means to be ordinary, but God makes extraordinary.

_____

_____

_____

3. Why are humility and grace important in your walk of faith?

_____

_____

_____

Daily Prayer

May our daily prayer be that we will seek Your ways, walk in Your paths, and be guided in truth so that we will learn of You and place our hope in You that we may be stable, secure, and faithful as You, Father, are faithful toward us. May we be strong in our relationship with You. May my story be about telling Your story. Lord, make us to be like Esther, Gideon, Paul, and others in the Bible, who walked in faith and trusted You even in the most difficult situations that could have ended in losing their lives. May we trust You even when we can't see the end of the story. Christ declares that we are triumphant in You. Lord, You are the victorious one in our lives. Amen.

"For the grace of God that bringeth salvation hath appeared to all men, teaching us that, denying ungodliness and worldly lusts, we should live soberly, righteously, and godly, in this present world; Looking for that blessed hope, and the glorious appearing of the great God and our Savior Jesus Christ" (Titus 2:11–13, KJV).

"And let the beauty of the Lord our God be upon us: and establish thou the work of our hands upon us; yea, the work of our hands establishes thou it" (Ps. 90:17, KJV).

DAY 27

Praying Grace

WHEN I THINK of praying grace, I am first reminded of the grace that is in my life. By definition: grace is the free and unmerited favor of God, as manifested in the salvation of sinners and the bestowal of blessings. For me personally, grace is strength, help in times of need, a force to be reckoned with, the overwhelming reckless love of God, compassion, all that I am not and all that He is, and the goodness of God. In addition, grace is His sacrifice that I might be saved, the extension of His favor and blessings. His grace covers me so that I can come into the presence of my God. But most of all, without grace, there would be no way to know Him as Lord and Savior. Without grace, we wouldn't know Him and be in a relationship with Him. For me, grace makes a way for me to come to Him. Praying for grace brings heaven's power to earth.

Prayer makes a way for me to be in relationship with my God. Through prayer, I can talk with Him, hear His voice, be led by Him, learn from Him, and grow in Him. Prayer can take many forms. You can be on your knees, on the floor on your face, standing tall with arms reaching high, sitting at His feet, walking in your garden or along the beach, or in a church building. You can pray to Him anywhere. The one thing He has made clear to me is that He is always ready to spend time with us in prayer. He is usually waiting on us to clear our schedules to meet with Him. A life of prayer makes the common uncommon. Prayer is the prerequisite for an ordinary life to become extraordinary.

There are many kinds of prayers. There is corporate prayer, like those who prayed together in the Upper Room in one accord to receive power and authority. There is corporate prayer when we pray together in a church service, at a conference, or in a small group. There is power in agreement in corporate prayer. There is just something so powerful about being in unity and agreement and standing together. It is like God hears us as one big powerful prayer reaching out to Him, and He cannot resist answering those prayers. I believe authentic, powerful, corporate prayers reach the throne of God and move Him.

I cannot imagine a life without having constant prayer. What is the first thing you do when there is a need? Is your automatic "go-to" prayer? Prayer opens doors, gives you courage to witness, and encourages and builds you up. It is His Spirit in you that rises and draws you to God and brings you to a place that is so intimate, so private, so personnel. It is a place where you and God meet alone. This time is priceless. Prayer is the door that opens to worship and anointing. It is through prayer with grace that we find the essence of God. Through prayer we also receive from God.

- When you pray, God listens.
- When you pray, storms are stilled.
- When you pray, doors open.
- When you pray, relationships get restored.
- When you pray, sicknesses get healed.
- When you pray, hope gets rekindled.
- When you pray, strength is renewed.
- When you pray, answers come.

Don't lose faith in what you are praying for today. God is faithful. His answers will come at just the right time. There are also prayers that are prayed using God's Word that are a reminder to us of His promises.

One of my favorite places to pray when I was in college was on the third floor of the library. There were dusty old reference books and rarely did anyone come into this section of the library. I could sit on the window-sill and have all the privacy I wanted and time to pray. I also cherished the time spent with precious Christian friends in the college prayer room early in the mornings and late into the evenings where we would pray together and see God's miraculous ways. This time spent in prayer with close friends changed my life and solidified a deep and personnel prayer walk with the Lord. I learned to pick up the things I had laid down and let God breathe life into them. Intercession brings about our assignments.

Through prayer you have impartation, fire, and authority. God wants to consume you like a fire. The one you spend your time with knows your voice, and you know His. You spend more time in prayer and reading the Bible because times are becoming more challenging. Awaken the fire of God in you. There are prayers of worship that we can see in the Psalms. Through prayer and worship comes anointing. Our passion goes to another level. We will have deeper love, deeper anointing, and experience God's presence as we spend time with Him in prayer and fasting.

"Call those things which are not as though they were" (Rom.4:17, NIV).

"Ask and you shall receive, seek and you shall find, knock and it will be opened" (Matt. 7:7, KJV). We are to ask and keep on asking, seek and keep on seeking, knock and keep on knocking. Remind yourself that we don't live by feelings, but by faith.

There are prayers of warfare. The enemy wants to disconnect us from the voice of God. We must get violent in our prayer closets and war rooms. Because of your prayers, others will be set free. "In all these things we were more than conquers through Him that loved us" (Rom. 8:37, NIV). God gives us a voice to call out to Him and declare His Word.

We should have the residue of God on us from being in His presence. We should be permeating with the fragrance of God. The presence of God is so lavishly given to us. Let us never become so accustomed to the presence of God that we don't see His fingerprints on our lives. Don't miss Jesus in His power when He is near but take that moment to encounter Him. Stop waiting for the King to show up on a white horse to rescue you. Don't just know Him from afar, from other's experiences. Open your eyes so that when He shows up, you will be sensitive to Him.

If we are going to see glory, we must have prayer in our lives. Draw near to the throne of God. We should burn for prayer. "He gives us the victory through Jesus Christ" (I Cor. 15:57, NIV). We are to pray, building ourselves up in faith (see Acts 2:42, NIV). When we are praying in the spirit, we are praying spirit to spirit. We are praying through our spirit to the Spirit of God. God is doing a work in us as we yield to Him in prayer. May our prayers and worship rise like incense to God.

> *"Every obstacle is an opportunity. Climbers see obstacles as opportunities. Climbers know that a bend in the road is not the end of the road!"*[36]

You will do for love what you would never do for duty. Your testimony is what God has done since you got saved. The love of God doesn't leave you like He found you. You are changed in His presence. You are a called out one. Your "yes" is significant. Do what God has called you to do. Will you dream God's dream for your life? It will cost you everything. But it is oh so worth it!

Dig a Little Deeper

1. Through prayer you have impartation, fire, and authority. Why are these elements important in your walk with the Lord?

_____

_____

_____

2. What does it mean when the scriptures indicate that we are to ask and keep on asking, seek and keep on seeking, knock and keep on knocking?

_____

_____

_____

3. Describe what happens when you pray.

_____

_____

_____

Daily Prayer

We pray that we will follow You, Lord, for You are more than what You can do for us. May our prayers be the faithful prayers of a righteous man/woman. Lord, lead us in Your grace. May we discover Your presence through prayer. Bend us, Lord, that we might know Calvary and that Your fire will consume us. Lord, may we believe for revival coming through prayer. May You hear our prayers and see our tears as we call out to You, and may You respond with power that revival of souls and miracles may transpire. Amen.

"Thou, therefore, my son, be strong in the grace
that is in Christ Jesus" (2 Tim. 2:1, KJV)

"Therefore, being justified by faith, we have
peace with God through our Lord Jesus Christ:
By whom also we have access by faith into this
grace wherein we stand and rejoice in hope
of the glory of God" (Rom. 5:1–2, KJV).

DAY 28

Sufficient Grace

W HEN OUR YOUNGEST son, Matthew, was a teenager, he and his
best friend, Chris, and a teenage girl were in his car out driving one
evening. The girl was in the back seat. Chris and Matt were in the front seat.
Matt was driving. The car in front of them hit their brakes and slid into the
car in front of them. Matt's car literally slid underneath the other car. Matt
did not have time to stop his car.

He hit the car in front of him, and he was also rear-ended. The impact
caused his gas tank to leak and caught on fire. Matt and Chris immediately
turned to the backseat and unlocked the girl's seat belt. The boys dove out
of the car as they opened the back door and pulled the girl out. In a matter
of seconds, the car exploded. The car was literally burned up inside and out.
Everything inside of the car melted because of the intensity of the fire.

The three of them got out safely without any harm. They smelled like
smoke, and the girl's hair smelled like it had been burned. We met the parents of the other two teenagers by the side of the road. Chris's dad said to
them, "You know the reason you all made it out of the car and are safe is
because God has a call on your lives. He protected you tonight." A little later,
the man driving the tow-truck stepped over to where we were and said, "I
have seen a lot of accidents, but none as bad as this one. The only way they
made it out of the car safely is because there was a fourth one in the car with
them." We knew with all certainty that night that God had protected our
child and his friends, and God's grace was sufficient in that moment.

It was the last two weeks before graduation from college. My heart was
in turmoil. I had prepared for four years to become a teacher. I was unsure of
where to go, what to do, and what was the next step for me to take. I spent
those two weeks fasting, and each night after everyone had gone to bed, I

would walk up and down the hallways and pray. Was I to go home? Was I to go somewhere for graduate school? What was God's will and plan for my life? I had believed there had been a call on my life to teach children and to be a missionary in India. But now, I was unsure of God's plan for me. Each night I would feel the Spirit of God drawing me close to Him. But I still didn't have my answer.

Then on the last night before graduation as I was praying, God spoke to me clearly. Without any reservation, I knew He was telling me to go home. This wasn't my expected answer. But I knew His voice, and I knew with all certainty this was His answer. There are times in our lives that we come to a crossroads and the decisions we make will determine not only our present but also our future. I went home and within a few months, I met my husband, and a year later we were married. Those two weeks of praying and fasting changed the course of my life. I will be forever grateful for God's guidance and sufficient grace during this time in my life.

We will never be sufficient in our own strength and abilities, but God gives us all that we need to fulfill what He calls us to do. His grace strengthens us in the middle of the call and gives us the grace to fulfill the call. In Romans, we see, "For by the grace given me I say to every one of you: Do not think of yourself more highly than you ought, but rather think of yourself with sober judgment in accordance with the measure of faith God has given you" (Rom. 12:3-4, NIV). We are commissioned to follow wholeheartedly. We see in Numbers the importance of following wholeheartedly: "Because they have not followed me wholeheartedly, not one of the men twenty years old or more who came up out of Egypt will see the land I promised an oath to Abraham, Isaac and Jacob" (Num. 32:11, NIV). God is our source of help. He gives us counsel and leads us in His ways. His grace is sufficient for the day.

If you can, imagine a small group of ten powerful, uncommon women meeting together with their mentor in a home in McKinney, Texas. They began to worship together. There was powerful revelation teaching. Then they began to pray together. The prayer ushered in an anointing, and our mentor began to wash the feet of each of us. The residue of this life was washed away. The sweet presence of God was undeniable, and the hearts in that room were quickened by the Spirit of God to hear what He was saying to each of us.

I am grateful for the grace of God to have been a part of this small group and the International Institute of Mentoring. I know that God was pouring into each of us what would be needed in the days ahead. God provides these unspeakable moments with Him to empower us, to humble us, to prepare us, to let us know He is with us, and He is sufficient. His sufficient grace is more than enough.

David's brothers saw him as a shepherd, but God saw him as a king. Let God define you and not others. When you walk in the identity God gives you, you are a victorious warrior. "You are defined by the love of one, His forgiveness and what He has done for you."[37] God gives you sufficient grace to live the life He has destined for you. When you hear that whisper in your ear that you are not enough, surely there is someone better to fulfill this vision; you ignore those whispers and continue to pursue after what God has called you to do or where He has called you to go. His grace is sufficient; it is more than enough. I have heard it said, the King of the world, whom heaven adores, the Lamb of Glory, the Lion of Judah believes in you and is cheering for you. You are strong in the Lord and the power of His might. You are qualified by Him, chosen by Him, and equipped by Him. Regardless of feelings, circumstances, overwhelming responsibilities, battles within, or without, you are an overcomer, and His grace is sufficient. We are world changers and history makers. We are the bride of Christ.

God will never allow more to be put on you than He puts within you to handle. The Psalmist tells us, "My soul (life) clings to you; your right hand upholds me" (Ps. 63:8, ESV). The power found in the personal relationship with Jesus Christ and His grace releases you from addictions and any stronghold on your life. You lose your fear when you know the power of being covered in grace. Sin will destroy you, and condemnation will fill you with unworthiness. However, grace and mercy are what Jesus displayed on the cross. Our pain is turned into purpose in His loving arms. God is looking for your "yes" to change the world. He chooses the weak and most unlikely. Because of our weaknesses, we are the most utterly dependent on God.

His grace is sufficient to make a way. All the while, God is at work on our behalf. Make God the most important love in your life and show Christ's love to one another. God protects, leads, and empowers us with His sufficient grace.

Dig a Little Deeper

1. You are qualified by Him, chosen by Him, and equipped by Him. Regardless of feelings, circumstances, overwhelming responsibilities, battles within or without, you are an overcomer, and His grace is sufficient. Write about a time in your life that you were solely dependent on God's sufficient grace.

_____

_____

_____

2. David's brothers saw him as a shepherd boy, but God had plans for David to be a king. Can you recall a time in your life that others didn't see your calling, but God was faithful to position you?

_____

_____

_____

3. What does it mean that God turns our pain into purpose?

_____

_____

_____

Daily Prayer

May our hearts be turned to your heart, Father, so that we would embrace your all-consuming love for us. Your grace, Lord, is sufficient for the day and everything we encounter throughout the day. May we ever be mindful of who You are and place our confident trust in You. You empower us to walk in Your sufficient grace. Amen.

"The Lord is not slack concerning His promise, as some men count slackness; but is longsuffering to us-ward, not willing that any should perish, but that all should come to repentance" (2 Pet. 3:9, KJV).

"For if ye turn again unto the Lord, your brethren and your children shall find compassion before them that lead them captive, so that they shall come again into this land: for the Lord, your God is gracious and merciful, and will not turn away His face from you, if ye return unto Him" (2 Chron. 30:9, KJV).

DAY 29

Redeeming Grace

AS I WAS driving home from work one day, I began to have severe cramps. I could continue to drive. I knew my doctor's office was nearby, so I continued to drive in my pain. They took a test and found that I was pregnant. I was in shock. We were not planning for another child. But of course, I was thankful for the news. But the pregnancy was ectopic. The baby was growing outside my uterus in my fallopian tubes. I was rushed to the hospital. There was no way the baby could survive, and if not operated on immediately, the baby could cause the tube to burst.

Everything happened so fast. I didn't really understand what was going on. I was rushed to the hospital and immediately taken to surgery where I lost the baby. I woke up from surgery filled with emotions, and I began crying. The doctor came into my room and asked why I was crying. She explained rather sarcastically that there was no way the fetus could have survived, and they were saving any chance for me to have another child.

But there was such an overwhelming grief in me for the loss of that child. Every fetus is a child, and every miscarriage is a lost child who should be grieved over. I found even in the middle of my grief that God's gentle grace comforted me and strengthened me. God took all my "what ifs" and reassured me that my baby was with Him. It was His redeeming grace that healed my soul.

I've heard it said, grace is the face love wears when it encounters imperfection. God's redeeming grace is applied to create pure hearts. It is with a pure heart that we bring pleasure to our Master. When we are broken, we receive His redeeming grace to make us new. Let us go back to the beginning of this book and recall the definition of grace. It is the free and unmerited favor of God, as manifested in the salvation of sinners and the bestowal of blessings.

Humility brings us to God's door, and grace opens that door. Paul's prayer was that we might be strengthened in our inner beings and that Christ might dwell in our hearts. "For this reason, I kneel before the Father, from whom His whole family in heaven and on earth derives its name. I pray that out of His glorious riches He may strengthen you with power through the spirit in your inner being, so that Christ may dwell in your hearts" (Eph. 3:14–16, NIV). He is pushing back the darkness for you. "Do not fear, for I have redeemed you; I have summoned you by name; you are mine" (Isa. 43:1, NIV).

God is aways there with His redeeming grace, ready to cover you and pull you close to Him. "I know that my Redeemer lives, and that in the end He will stand on the earth" (Job 19:25, NIV). The psalmist encourages us to put our hope in the Lord and His unfailing love, for in Him we find redemption. "O Israel put our hope in the Lord, for with the Lord is unfailing love and with Him is full redemption" (Ps. 130:7, NIV). Grace empowers us to walk in what has been given to us. He says that He knows the plans He has for you, and they are to prosper you, plans for a good future, plans to give you an expected and beautiful end (see Jer. 29:11, NIV).

Ruth's kinsman redeemer is a foreshadowing of Jesus, our Kinsman Redeemer. We see God's grace extended over and over to Ruth until she is finally redeemed. Ruth's story begins with a choice made by her father-in-law Elimelech. He decided to leave "The House of Bread," Bethlehem, for there was famine in the land, to go to Moab, named after one of Lot's sons. Ruth and Boaz's story is a love story of God's providential care. This is a story of provision and choices that determined fulfilled destiny. God takes Elimelech's bad choice and, after his death, brings redemption.

Mahlon and his family were originally from Bethlehem, Judah. He and his family went to Moab due to a famine. Ruth had originally married Mahlon, the son of Elimelech and Naomi. When her husband Mahlon and her father-in-law Elimelech died, Ruth traveled to Bethlehem with her mother-in-law Naomi. According to Mosaic Law, if a woman's husband died and she was without children, her husband's brother was required to marry her so there could be an heir to carry on the name of the man who had died (see Deut. 25:5–6, NIV).

If she had never married Mahlon entering this Jewish household, she would not have had the opportunity to return to Bethlehem. God's plan for her life was to bring redemption to her and her heirs, even though she did not know all that would come about because of her choice or how her choice would affect her offspring. The nearest kinsman would have the first option to marry Ruth. He refused because marrying Ruth would place his own children's inheritance at risk if he and Ruth had children. Ruth and Boaz participated in a redeeming transaction. Boaz then became her kinsman redeemer. Ruth is the great-grandmother of King David and named in the genealogy of Jesus (see the book of Ruth and Matt., chapter 1).

"Fear not, for I have redeemed you; I have called you by name. You are mine" (Isa. 43:1, NIV). "Because of the Lord's great love, we are not consumed, for His compassions never fail. They are new every morning; great is your faithfulness. I say to myself, The Lord is my portion, therefore I will wait for Him" (Lam. 3:22–24, NIV).

This is a story of redemption. Boaz, an uncommon man, is a foreshadowing of Jesus our Redeemer, Deliverer, Mighty God. When our breath has been knocked out of us, He breathes life into us. God wrote our stories long before we lived them. Whatever is taking place in your life, wherever you may currently be in your life, God has you in the palm of His hands, and He is perfecting you! If you are feeling inadequate, humble yourself. Let humility lead you and lean into Him for courage, insight, and direction.

If you are not doing something that feels impossible, you are not chasing after all God has for you. If it is not hard, if it doesn't require something of you, it is probably not worth it. If you are going through a rough time, don't despair. This may just be the end of your current chapter. Look forward to the next chapter. This is your story that only you can tell. Let God write His story of His redeeming grace on your heart.

Dig a Little Deeper

1. Can you think of a time that God's redeeming grace has protected you?

   _____

   _____

   _____

2. Have you ever been overwhelmed by life and found yourself dependent on God to help you through this season?

   _____

   _____

   _____

3. Do you know Jesus as your Redeemer? How has He redeemed you?

   _____

   _____

   _____

Daily Prayer

We pray that daily we will cling to You, Kinsman Redeemer, Jesus. May we never lose sight of the price You paid to redeem us and realize Your dreams in us. May Your redeeming grace draw us close to You. May Your redeeming grace bring humility and strength to us. Your redeeming grace breathes life into lost dreams and visions. We know our Redeemer lives. You live in us. May Your grace redeem all that has been dead and bring new life into those situations and lives. Amen.

"The grace of our Lord Jesus Christ be with
your spirit. Amen" (Philemon 1:25, KJV).

"To the praise of the glory of his grace, wherein he
hath made us accepted in the beloved" (Eph. 1:6, KJV).

DAY 30

Unmerited Grace

TODAY, AS I was getting into my car to drive to the women's correctional facility, God reminded me of this scripture. "Don't be afraid, for I am with you. Don't be discouraged, for I am your God. I will strengthen you and help you. I will hold you up with my victorious right hand" (Isa. 41:10, NKJV). I had been in the juvenile facility many times, but this was my first time to be at the "Big Jail," as the teens like to call it. Three other Gideon women greeted me. The four of us waited outside until the prison doors were unlocked for us to enter. We prayed as we waited.

The twelve Gideon men had brought in boxes of Bibles they were taking to the men's area. We each filled our arms with Bibles to carry into the women behind those locked doors. We were patted down, and all personal items placed in a locked area. My heart began to race as we walked through the unlocked doors that slammed closed and locked behind us. We walked down a long hallway past the men's cafeteria and the laundry area. My head began to swim with a vivid imagination, remembering every prison movie I had ever seen. But there was no Morgan Freeman or any other movie star behind those glass windows and locked doors. These men were the ages of my sons, and God quickly reminded me that He brings hope to the hopeless. So, I prayed for them as the four of us and the guard walked past them.

We walked to "G" area. The guard unlocked the first door, and we walked into a small holding area with another locked door in front of us as the door behind us slammed shut. We had come to distribute Bibles. I was the only unseasoned one in the group. So, I stayed close to the back of the group and watched what the other ladies did or said. I looked up, and painted in red on the wall was the word GRACE. This represented "G" area. I felt a sudden release in my spirit, and I knew God had brought us here on an assignment. Yes, we were there to give each one a Bible and possibly lead them through the salvation plan in the back of the Bible, but God was already at work in that room.

We walked in with our boxes and arms full of Bibles to bring to these women all dressed in brown jumpsuits. There were several guards around the room. We passed the place where they showered, and I thought about how they had no privacy. The little rooms where they lived and shared with a roommate were hardly big enough to turn around. The women inmates were all sitting in chairs, facing a woman who was sharing the gospel with them. She was reading out of 1st Corinthians 13 and then shared about the love of God. I looked around the room at the faces of these women, wondering if there would be one I knew. Most of them looked so young. As I watched their faces, my heart began to break for each of them, and my eyes teared up. None of them would have chosen to be there, and I knew it was only by the grace of God that I wasn't among them. If not for Jesus in my life, where would I be?

After the woman had finished ministering, we all made a circle and prayed together. Then we gave out the Bibles. I could feel a release in my spirit. God had a plan, and if I would just yield myself to Him, He would meet this day with these women. They were receptive, and each was eager to have her own Bible. We prayed for recovery from addictions, their children and families, and for them to have the strength to not go back to their previous lives. I held their hands and wrapped my arms around them. I looked in their eyes and let them know they were loved, and that God was with them even in that place. With tears in their eyes, they thanked me, and I knew Jesus had met them where they were this day.

As we left and the doors slammed shut, I could still see each of their faces. As I drove home, tears flowed down my face as I prayed for them. There was a heaviness in my heart. God spoke to me in my spirit, and I knew that His heart was broken for these women who were in the valley of decision, caught somewhere between knowing God's faithfulness and trusting Him, and then fighting the memories of who they had been and all they had done. God reminded me of His great love for all His daughters and that our prayers carry them in these times.

A God kind of grace is a gift that is given without any merit. We don't deserve it, but He gives it anyway. God knows the very depths of us and continues to love us. The Psalmist describes the close relationship God desires to have with us:

> "O Lord, you have searched me and know me. You know when I sit and when I rise, you perceive my thoughts from afar. You discern my going out and my lying down, you are familiar with all my ways, before a word is on my tongue you know it completely, O Lord. You hem me in—behind and before, you have laid your hand upon me. Such knowledge is too wonderful for me, too lofty for me to attain. Where can I go from your Spirit? Where can I flee from your presence? If I go up to the heavens, You are there; If I make my bed in the depths, You are there. If I rise on the wings of the dawn, if I settle on the far side of the sea, even there your hand will guide me, your right hand will hold me fast." (Ps. 139:1–10, NIV)

It is a mystery that one could encompass so great a love as our heavenly Father has toward us. How is it that Jesus could give so willingly, so freely of Himself for us? Such love is incomprehensible. Who am I that He would choose to love me to such depths? This love is unfathomable. He has poured His love on us through Calvary, and daily, He extends His love to us with outreached arms that say, "I am here for you." He calls the weary to come and lay their heads in His lap. He calls the heartbroken to be comforted in His outstretched arms. He calls the weary to sit at His feet. He calls us friend then He walks beside us. All that we are or ever hope to be is because of this great love that He has chosen to pour on us. We are reminded in Ephesians of God's great love for us:

"But because of His great love for us, God who is rich in mercy, made us alive with Christ even when we were dead in transgressions—it is by grace you have been saved. And God raised us up with Christ and seated us with Him in the heavenly realms in Christ Jesus, in order that in the coming ages he might show the incomparable riches of His grace, expressed in His kindness to us in Christ Jesus. For it is by grace you have been saved, through faith—and this not from yourselves, it is the gift of God—not by works, so that no one can boast. For we are God's workmanship. Created in Christ Jesus to do good works, which God prepared in advance for us to do." (Eph. 2:4–10, NIV).

Love came down, and mankind was forever changed. God's unmerited grace has been poured out for us.

Dig a Little Deeper

1. Have you ever been in the valley of decision in between knowing God's faithfulness and trusting him?

_____

_____

_____

2. Explain what it means that God brings hope to the hopeless.

_____

_____

_____

3. What does it mean that it is a mystery that one could encompass so great a love as our heavenly Father has toward us?

_____

_____

_____

Daily Prayer

Father, fill us with Your unmerited grace that we might extend Your grace to others. Lord, fill us with compassion and mercy for the lost and hopeless. Place in us grace that we can look others in their eyes, and they will see You in our eyes. We don't deserve Your grace, but we are oh so thankful for it. Hold us close to You and mend our brokenness. Empty us of ourselves and fill us with all that is You. May we extend grace to this broken and cruel world that the lost and hopeless will find You. It is with a grateful heart that we have the privilege of knowing You and following You. Amen.

"For our rejoicing is this, the testimony of our conscience, that in simplicity and godly sincerity, not with fleshly wisdom, but by the grace of God, we have had our conversation in the world, and more abundantly to you-ward" (2 Cor. 1:12, KJV).

"Wherefore gird up the loins of your mind, be sober, and hope to the end for the grace that is to be brought unto you at the revelation of Jesus Christ" (1 Pet. 1:13, KJV).

DAY 31

Finding Grace

A S I WALKED up the mountain side of Assisi, Italy, I could see rows of grapes staked to the wooden posts and stretched across the wire lines. On one side, you could see the plump juicy grapes, and on the other side you could see the olive groves. At the top of the mountain is a church where the early Christians had met. What an honor to sit where they had sat and pray where they had prayed, knowing their personal walk with the Lord might require their lives. The monks live in the facilities there at Assisi. They take care of the fields. Assisi is one of my favorite places to visit, not just for its beauty, but for the spirit you can feel there as the prayers are constantly sent forth to God like a fresh incense going up to the heavens.

The prize-winning wine is the best wine because the grapes were on the vine longer. These grapes are bigger, richer, sweeter, and fuller. The fragrance is sweet, and the color clear but full bodied. This would be the good wine offered by Jesus that represented His blood, the wine saved until last at the wedding feast. Sometimes before He can even begin the process in us, we abort what He has designed to be birthed in us. If we choose to separate ourselves from the vine with the first wind that blows, the first storm, or because we are uncomfortable, we stop the process that we must go through to be all God has purposed us to be and do. We may have many dreams, many callings, many giftings, many desires; but if we are unwilling to stay connected to the vine and go through the process to the end, we are preventing the Lord of the Harvest to prepare us and change us, create in us, make us to be what His original design was intended to be for us. As we go through the process, we find grace. Jesus says:

"I am the true vine, and my father is the vinedresser. Every branch in me that does not bear fruit he takes away; and every branch that bears fruit he prunes, that it may bear more fruit. You are already clean because of the words which I have spoken you. Abide in me, and I in you. As the branch cannot bear fruit of itself, unless it abides in the vine, neither can you, unless you abide in Me. I am the vine; you are the branches. He who abides in me, and I in him bears much fruit, for without me you can do nothing. If anyone does not abide in me, he is thrown away like a branch and is withered; and the branches are gathered, thrown into the fire, and burned. If you abide in me, and my words abide in you, ask whatever you wish, and it will be done for you. By this my Father is glorified that you bear much fruit, so you will be my disciples" (John 15:1–8, NIV).

Vineyards require great care. They require pruning and watering to make them remain healthy and strong. The vineyard's beginning starts with one healthy strong root from another vineyard, and in time, that root will produce branches and fruit that begins to grow. Then, from that main branch, they will cut off a piece to plant to grow more plants. Eventually, after years from the first cutting off from the main vine, and replanting many times, you would have a vineyard. The vineyard is only as strong as the original root and the richness of the soil. Then as they grow, branches grow or intertwine themselves with the branches. That was when pruning took place. It is during this process that we find grace. This entails a process of cutting away the unproductive branch so that it would not take the nutrients from the soil that the original roots would need to produce a good harvest. The vine must be pruned to survive and thrive. The result is a blessed harvest and many times more grapes than there were previously.

Jesus says to us in the book of John, "You did not choose me, but I chose you and appointed you to go and bear fruit—fruit that will last. Then the Father will give you whatever you ask in my name" (John 15:16, NIV). I have heard it said, "He is the root extractor and seed planter." The Lord of the harvest has planted a vineyard that will yield a vintage harvest. The best harvest will be determined by the root going deep, making it strong and healthy, and the right amount of sap is running in the veins of the vine. We must pull up those roots that don't belong in the vineyard; those things that are keeping us from growing up. We must prepare the oil lamps to prevent frost, and the season must be long enough to produce a fully developed harvest.

The Lord of the Harvest is watching over the harvest until it is fully developed—full flavored, plump, juicy, mature, ready to be harvested. Premature harvesting results in a failed harvest. The process of making wine is a process that reflects the work the Holy Spirit does in us.

There is a waiting time when we draw close to the vine and remain attached, dependent on the vine. If we want to bear good fruit, we must abide in the vine. We need to stay close to the vine to become mature. Rich, ready fruit is then plucked from the vine at the right time, and then the fruit is taken to the winepress. If the grape does not stay in the press, then the seeds, peelings, things that need to be stripped away are not taken away. The fruit stays in the press until the juice is separated from the rest of the fruit. God is with us in the time of pressing. When we are pressed, God is taking out the things holding us back from Him. We must choose to stay until His work is finished in us. Quitting is not an option. We move from comfortable to uncomfortable. Mature ones who are connected to the vine are not consumed or overwhelmed or distracted by the circumstance. The winepress represents the things we go through in life and how if we yield ourselves to God, He takes out the parts of us that doesn't produce good fruit while keeping the good part of the fruit.

The good wine offered by Jesus represents His blood; this was the wine saved until last at the wedding feast. It has a sweet fragrance. This is symbolic of Jesus pouring Himself out for us and the Holy Spirit dwelling in us. We must follow the process to the end to find His grace. The fields are white unto harvest, and we are called to be laborers of this harvest. He saved the best for last. It is time *now* to bring in the harvest!

Dig a Little Deeper

1. Just as the grapes on the vine must go through a process to be fully developed, we go through a process to find grace. What is the process we must go through to find grace?

    _____

    _____

    _____

2. Compare the relationship between the vine and the branch to our relationship with Christ Jesus.

    _____

    _____

    _____

3. What does it mean to be a seed planter and the root extractor?

    _____

    _____

    _____

Daily Prayer

Father, let our daily prayer be that we are yours. May we be vines that are connected to the branch, Jesus, and may we bear good fruit. Teach us, Lord, to prune and extract the things in our lives that need to be removed to move us closer to You. Lord, may our lives yield a great harvest and may we know the times and seasons to bring in the harvest of souls for Your kingdom's sake. At the end of our story, may our heavenly Father say, "Well done." Amen.

AFTERWORD

Thirty-One Days to Learn the Secret of Walking in Grace

YOU HAVE A destiny and a call for your life. To fulfill God's purpose for your life, you must first walk in grace. God did not call you to be common, but to live an uncommon life. He did not call you to be ordinary. He called you to be extraordinary through His grace. Put His super on your natural for you to become supernatural. I have heard it said, step out of the ordinary zone and step into the miracle zone. He is calling you to go out into the harvest fields and tell the world about Jesus Christ and His saving grace. He is the one, the only true God, who by His grace saves, forgives, and gives eternal life. Jesus's death on the cross is the supreme act of grace. Jesus exemplifies grace through giving Himself to redeem us from our sins. We should have been the ones on that cross. But He took our place and saved us from the death that would have come from our sins.

He asks only for your "yes." Then He makes a way when there seems to be no way. He redeems you by His grace that is sufficient, sustaining, supernatural, anointed, and authentic, amazing, and everlasting. Grace is a gift, and it is unrelenting and empowering. You are ambassadors of God's grace. It is by His uncommon grace that you are empowered to live an uncommon life.

There is a secret to walking in grace that is required to live this empowered, uncommon life. This secret is simply to abide in God's presence. His presence brings you from the common to the uncommon, from victim to victor, from the powerless to the powerful. His presence breaks through unforgiveness, brokenness, and brings healing. In his presence, we find His grace. You can't abide in His presence without first knowing His grace.

Once you dwell in His presence, you can then walk out His grace. Once you have experienced His grace in your life, then you can extend His grace to others. Surrender your life to Jesus Christ and walk in His grace. We are to extend a place of grace within the body of Christ and for everyone, no matter their past sins or present challenges. Jesus chose the least of the least. Paul killed Christians. Peter denied Christ. They were ordinary men, sinful men, called out to follow Christ. It was their "yes" to follow Jesus that brought grace into their lives.

Grace also makes a place for us no matter what we have done or where we have been; all we need to do is to choose Jesus. Follow Jesus and extend His grace to others. May the light of Jesus in you invade the dark places in others. When you received salvation, you received grace (see Acts 19). Since you were saved, have you received more grace? Since your failures, have you received grace? It only requires your yes and dwelling in His presence to know His grace. We are uncommon ordinary people. We need his grace in our lives every day. It is grace that makes us uncommon and extraordinary.

> "But He said to me, 'My grace is sufficient for you, for my power is made perfect in weakness.' Therefore, I will boast all the more gladly about my weaknesses, so that Christ's power may rest on me" (2 Cor. 12:9, NIV).

Bibliography

Dick, Lois Hoadley. *Amy Carmichael: Let the Little Children Come.* Chicago: The Moody Bible Institute, Copyright © 1984. p. 20–21, 123, 111, 150. ISBN 0–8024–0433–2.

Hayford, Jack W. *The Hayford Bible Handbook.* Nashville, Tennessee: Thomas Nelson Publishing, © 1995. The Complete Companion for Spirit-Filled Bible Study. Thomas Nelson is a registered trademark of Harper Collins Christian Publishing, Inc. pp. 543–544. ISBN 978–0-310–13413–8.

Jacobs, Judy. *Pray Until.* Shippensburg, PA: Destiny Image Publishers, Inc. Copyright 2022. p. 18. ISBN 13: 978–0-7684–6309–5. Pastor Jack Hayford said, *"Prayer is invading the impossible."* (*Pray Until,* Destiny Image © 2022: Judy Jacobs, p.18).

Jacobs, Judy. *Stand Strong.* Lake Mary, Florida: Charisma House Publishing. Copyright ©2007. ISBN 978–1-59979–066–4.

Jacobs, Judy. *You Are Anointed for This.* Charisma Media/Charisma House Book Group 600 Rinehart Road Lake Mary, Florida: Copyright © 2013. ISBN 978–1-62136–282–1.

Johnson, Bill. *Hosting the Presence.* Shippensburg, PA: Destiny Image Publishers, Inc.© Copyright 2012 pp. 19, 74. ISBN 13 TP: 978–0-7684–4129–1.

Kinkade, Thomas. *Glorious Refrains.* Thomas Nelson Publishing. © Copyright 2002. Morgan Hill, CA. pp.13, 22.

Morehead, Philip D, & Morehead, Andrew T. *Roget's College Thesaurus in Dictionary Form.* Copyright © 1985. Third Edition.

Endnotes

1. Helen Lemmel, "Turn Your Eyes Upon Jesus," 1922.

2. Judy Jacobs quoting Charles Spurgeon, International Institute of Mentoring (IIOM), Facebook IIOM Teaching, 2022. (https://www.facebook.com/MentorMeIIOM/)

3. Judy Jacobs, Quote, International Institute of Mentoring (IIOM), Facebook IIOM Teaching, 2022. (https://www.facebook.com/MentorMeIIOM/)

4. Bill Johnson, *Hosting the Presence* (Shippensburg: Destiny Image Publishers, 2012), 19, 74.

5. Judy Jacobs, Quote, International Institute of Mentoring (IIOM), Facebook IIOM Teaching, 2018. (https://www.facebook.com/MentorMeIIOM/)

6. Judy Jacobs, Sermon, Dwelling Place Church, 2019.

7. Ibid.

8. Rhonda Guiles Davis, Sermon, Facebook, 2022. (https://www.facebook.com/DaystarTV/videos/ministry-now-with-rhonda-guiles-davis/452018332963567/?locale=ms_MY)

9. Thomas Kinkade, *Glorious Refrains* (Morgan Hill: Thomas Nelson Publishing, 2002), 13, 22.

10. Daniel Fusco, Daystar TV Sermon at Crossroads Community Church, 2022, Day Star Television.

11. Charisma Staff, "Judy Jacobs: What's So Great About the Anointing?", *Charisma Magazine,* July 22, 2013, https://charismamag.com/spiritled-living/supernaturaldreams/what-s-so-great-about-the-anointing/.

12. Judy Jacobs, Quote, International Institute of Mentoring (IIOM), Facebook IIOM Teaching, 2022. (https://www.facebook.com/MentorMeIIOM/)

13. Judy Jacobs quoting Jonathan Edwards, International Institute of Mentoring (IIOM), Facebook IIOM Teaching, 2022. (https://www.facebook.com/MentorMeIIOM/)

14. Judy Jacobs, *Pray Until* (Shippensburg: Destiny Image Publishers, 2022), 18.

15. (Jeremiah Johnson, (2-20-2022). (https://www.jeremiahjohnson.tv)

16. Chuck Swindoll, Sermon, Daystar TV, 2022, Television.

17. Billy Graham, Sermon, Billy Graham Ministries, Facebook, 2020.

18. Deleted Reference #18 quote from John Bevere from text.

19. Christine Caine, Sermon, Daystar TV, 2022, Television.

20. Judy Jacobs, *Stand Strong* (Lake Mary: Charisma House Publishing, 2007), 169-170.

21. Lois Hoadley Dick, *Amy Carmichael: Let the Little Children Come* (Chicago: The Moody Bible Institute, 1984), 20-21, 111, 123, 150.

22. Judy Jacobs, *You Are Anointed for This* (Lake Mary: Charisma Media/Charisma House Book Group, 2031), 25.

23. Judy Jacobs, Quote, International Institute of Mentoring (IIOM), Facebook IIOM Teaching, 2020. (https://www.facebook.com/MentorMeIIOM/)

24. Jacobs, *You Are Anointed for This*, 23.

25. Jack W. Hayford, *The Hayford Bible Handbook* (Nashville: Thomas Nelson Publishing, 1995), 543-544.

26. Johnson, *Hosting the Presence*, 23.

27. Jacobs, *You Are Anointed for This*, 25.

28. Judy Jacobs quoting Corrie Ten Boom, International Institute of Mentoring (IIOM), Facebook IIOM Teaching, 2022. (https://www.facebook.com/MentorMeIIOM/)

29. Judy Jacobs, Quote, International Institute of Mentoring (IIOM), Facebook IIOM Teaching, 2022. (https://www.facebook.com/MentorMeIIOM/)

30. Johnson, *Hosting the Presence,* 81.

31. Robert Lowry, "Nothing But the Blood of Jesus," 1876.

32. Rhonda Guiles Davis, Sermon, Facebook, 2022. (https://www.facebook.com/DaystarTV/videos/ministry-now-with-rhonda-guiles-davis/452018332963567/?locale=ms_MY)

33. Thomas Kinkade, *Glorious Refrains* (Morgan Hill: Thomas Nelson Publishing, 2002), 13, 22.

34. Jamie Tuttle, Sermon, Dwelling Place Church, Cleveland, TN, 2022.

35. Sundar Sadhu Singh, "I Have Decided to Follow Jesus," 1889.

36. Jentezen Franklin, Climbers Sermon, Daystar TV, 2022, Television.

37. Samuel Rodriguez, Sermon, Oasis Church, Los Angeles, May 2023.

Printed in the USA
CPSIA information can be obtained
at www.ICGtesting.com
JSHW010244071123
51582JS00003B/13